Your Pets Are Fine ...and Other Lies

True Adventures in Pet Sitting

YVONNE M. FELTMAN

ISBN 10: 0-9990109-0-5 (print)
ISBN 13: 978-0-9990109-0-7 (print)
ISBN 10: 0-9990109-1-3 (eBook)
ISBN 13: 978-0-9990109-1-4 (eBook)
Library of Congress Control Number: 2017909438

Interior design by Yvonne M. Feltman
Cover design by Iva23 - ivaozi23@gmail.com
Author photo by Aaron Husak

I dedicate this book to the friends and family members who have listened to me talk about it for far longer than it took me to write it. I finally did it!

This is also for all of the dogs and cats I've cared for over the years. You've taught me lessons I needed to learn.

Lastly, this is for Jiminey Cricket, my beloved dog who passed away not long ago. Thank you for expanding my capacity to love more than I ever could have imagined.

CONTENTS

Preface   *i*

1   Introduction   1

2   Blood, Saliva, Tears, and Terror (Fourth of July)   11

3   The Horrible Helper and the Lost Cat   19

4   Lost and Found, and Kept   29

5   A Killer Next Door   47

6   Pet Sitting for a Local Celebrity   63

7   The Toilet Water Flood   71

8   They'll Never Know   79

9   Illegals Living in the Backyard   87

10   Celebrity Guest   99

11   Hide Your Valuables – I Mean, Hide Your Food   113

12   I'm a House Sitter, Not a Homewrecker!   119

13   The First Bite is the Deepest   131

14   Where's the Fire?   139

Epilogue   145

Acknowledgments   147

About the Author   149

PREFACE

The stories in this book are based on actual true events in my life. These took place in Albuquerque, New Mexico and Austin, Texas. Some stories are more loosely truth-based than others. For privacy purposes, I have changed most names and some identifying details.

1
INTRODUCTION

"Are you done with pet sitting now or what?" was a friend's response when I told her I decided to reveal all of my crazy pet sitting experiences in a book. She was implying that by telling the true stories contained herein, no one would want to hire me ever again. She could be right. Call me brave or stupid, but someone needs to tell these stories that have undoubtedly been experienced by other pet sitters in some degree or another. Or maybe it was only me, but somehow I doubt it.

I began pet sitting years ago while I was in college in Albuquerque, New Mexico. My twin sister, Kellie, had been pet sitting for her coworkers, and when she wasn't available to cover a trip, she referred me to them. It was then that my pet sitting side hustle began. That first client led to another, then another, and another. Word-of-mouth steadily grew my business. Eventually, in 2006, I decided to create a website, join the local pet sitters' organization, and form a legit Limited Liability Company (LLC). I pet sat for many years while working full-time in a corporate office as an Executive Assistant. Tired of the corporate hum-drum, a few years ago I decided to make pet sitting my main source of income.

Pet sitting can't be a significant source of income if one is horrible at it. And trust me, after several years of lint-brush mastery, poop scooping, and dog walking, I can safely claim to be a professional pet sitter. I may even be good at it. I could explain to you all the ways to be a great sitter, but instead, I think I'd rather showcase the ways in which I've failed miserably. I promise it will make you feel better about your own failures.

I will admit that it was somewhat traumatic writing this book and experiencing my grand failures, flukes, and strange encounters all over again. I've debated whether or not to share these stories because some aren't all that funny. A few are downright wretched. After the experience in a few chapters, especially chapter five, you will understand why I later experienced symptoms of post-traumatic stress disorder (PTSD).

Anyone who has ever found a pet sitter they are pleased with probably has stories about a few prior sitters who were less than stellar. I've heard some awful stories from new clients that began with,

"Our old pet sitter did..." and they rattle off stories about their past pet sitter's chaos and neglect. When meeting new clients, I try to never tell them that I am not all that surprised about those prior bad experiences. As you'll soon discover, I've had my own bouts of unfortunate pet sitting events sprinkled over several years.

It is strangely comforting to know that I am not alone. If it is possible to feel appalled and empathetic at the same time, it happens to me each time I receive an industry email from the provider of my pet sitters insurance. Most pet sitters and pet sitting companies have pet sitters insurance in case a mishap occurs. The periodic email they send includes recent pet sitter claims, payouts, and other pet industry tidbits. While it is probably a scare tactic to get me to keep my pet sitting insurance, the email always lends a stark reminder of the things that can go wrong while pet sitting:

- Client dog attempted to eat a baited hook while being walked by the member near a bay; vet care was required to remove hook from the dog's mouth - $460 paid

- Member let client dog out in a thunderstorm; dog got skittish, broke free from leash and ran off; dog was found injured; vet care was required - $2950 paid

- Five-month-old puppy was on-leash in member's car and jumped out of the window; required medical attention - $889 paid

- Client dog was left unattended in the member's car; dog ate a bag of dog treats; dog's stomach ruptured and vet care was required - $10,095 paid

- Client dog ate a mini-tennis ball while off-leash at the park with the member; required surgery - $3630 paid

- Pet sitter contractor was walking client dog on-leash; dog jumped on third party person who was bitten, required medical attention and income from missed work - $1930 paid

- Client reported missing jewelry and money after pet sitter contractor was caring for client pets - $5870 paid

- Client dog soiled the carpet repeatedly when in the care of the member and a pet sitter contractor; professional carpet cleaning was required - $506 paid

- Member didn't latch the screen door properly at the client's home; wind broke the hinges and the door needed to be replaced - $140 paid

- Pet sitter contractor lost the keys to five client homes; some clients wanted their homes to be re-keyed - $386 paid

These claims demonstrate the reasons why I've stayed a small company with only a handful of pet sitter contractors: less liability. That doesn't mean that bad things don't happen—you can read about one of the bad pet sitter contractors I've had in chapter three. It's one thing to be responsible for my own behavior, but to risk my business reputation by being responsible for many other people's potential bad decisions is frankly not worth the trouble. Sometimes, staying a small business is a good thing.

Even when staying small, accidents happen to the best of us. One time I cooked a pizza at a client's home. When the pizza was done, I took it out of the oven and rested it atop the stove so it could cool off. While it cooled, I briefly used the restroom down the hall. Imagine my surprise two minutes later when I returned to find half the pizza devoured by the dog, a Blue Heeler, who had previously been asleep in the living room, uninterested in what I was doing in the kitchen. I was able to salvage some of the pizza to eat, and I was lucky that the dog seemed unfazed by its impromptu Italian dinner.

Then there was the time, not long ago, when I arrived at a client's home in the middle of nowhere outside of Austin, Texas. I had met their two dogs during two meet-and-greets at their house in the weeks prior. The owners were on their flight out and

I had arrived in the afternoon to start my stay. When I unlocked the front door, their larger dog decided not to welcome me warmly, or even act like she knew me. With the dog inches away from me, she lunged at me, barking viciously. I noticed her pupils were dilated and she was becoming fixated on me as if I was her prey. Flashbacks from watching the movie Cujo as a child raced through my mind. All I could think about was that I would get attacked and die there on that porch in the woods. I probably wouldn't be discovered for days. To my surprise, she managed to calm down as she was able to familiarize with my scent in the fifteen seconds that I stood there paralyzed by fear. The rest of my stay went off without a hitch, but it was another reminder that canines can be unpredictable.

Something that is predictable though, is the curiosity that people have about this vocation. For this reason, I try to fly under the radar when meeting new people, because I don't love to carry on about myself. I am more interested in what others have to say. To my dismay, at a recent women's charity event, we were instructed to introduce ourselves right off the bat to the others at our table, and tell them what we do for a living.

"Hi, my name is Yvonne Feltman, and I own a pet sitting company here in Austin. I am also in the final stages of publishing a book." If I was going to have to reveal my profession, I might as well try to promote my pending book, right?

"Really? That is great! What is your book about?" A college-aged woman whose nametag read "Emily" perked up, smiling warmly.

"It is a book about my pet sitting adventures. There is some humor, some chaos and some other crazy situations I've experienced while pet sitting," I said, making eye-contact with Emily and each woman around the table. The table buzzed with approval and chatter.

Then another woman raised her hand slightly as if we were in a classroom and asked, "What made you decide to write a book?"

"Whenever I meet people, I try not to be forthcoming about being a pet sitter—I never want to come across sales-y. However, when they discover what I do, there is naturally a lot of curiosity and questions. So after years of this, it dawned on me that I should write a book about my experiences," I said, bracing myself for said questions.

Sure enough, the usual questions were asked:

"So you stay in people's homes overnight? You actually sleep in their bed?"

"Yes, I do. Most of the time I sleep in their bed, the sheets are clean, of course. Many times people have a guest bed, so I'll sleep there."

"How much do you charge?"

"I start at sixty dollars per night which includes care for up to two pets," I explained.

"How long have you been pet sitting?"

"Fifteen years on the side, the last few years of which it has been a main source of income."

After a few more questions and lively conversation, I pointed out to the group that this was the very reason why I was writing a book about pet sitting—the level of curiosity! I explained that one day I can simply say, "Buy my book," when I sense a rapid-fire question session about to begin. Everyone laughed because it was not untrue. Hopefully, some of those women actually bought this book and are laughing now, as they read this.

Anyway, one of the questions I got that day and often is, "Do you ever have to turn anyone down?" I wish I could say no, but just as there are bad pet sitters, there are iffy clients as well.

I once showed up for a meet-and-greet at a house in a nice neighborhood. The home seemed perfectly normal on the outside, had great curb appeal. When I entered the home it was immediately apparent that hoarders lived there. They had three dogs and three cats. After taking the tour of their cluttered home, with floor to ceiling junk stacked throughout, I felt like I could barely breathe. I decided that the crippling claustrophobia I'd inevitably endure while staying there was not worth taking on the client. I felt bad when I politely turned them down a couple of days later.

At a different meet-and-greet, there was the big mutt who hungrily fixated on my little Miniature Pinscher, Jiminey. Her name was Betty and I wasn't sure if she wanted to play or bite as she sniffed him and whimpered eagerly. Betty's owners had a sitter cancel at the last minute, so they were scrambling to find another pet sitter for their vacation the following week. Back then, Jiminey would stay with me on all of my pet sits, so I brought him along on all of my meet-and-greets, too. At this one, I would not let Jiminey out of my arms for fear that Betty would eat him like the squirrel she seemed to think he was. Due to her size, it would take one bite from her and he'd be gone. Spending a week at the house separating the two was not fair to either dog, so I had to decline that client too.

Then there are the high-maintenance clients who literally want you to walk, run, bathe, massage, groom, entertain, take on trips to the dog park, wipe butts, scrub paws, clean teeth, floss teeth, cook for, vacuum daily, serenade, rock to sleep, wake up at 5 A.M. each day, go on multiple hour-long walks, and then send them non-stop photo updates of their pets. And they want all that for the rate of $19 per day. I'm exaggerating, but you get my drift. It is amazing when clients demand I treat their dog like a Kardashian and they pay me like a bus boy. It is a good thing that I can recognize those types a mile away, and can steer clear!

Even with occasionally undesirable clients and random mishaps, pet sitting is rewarding and fun. The cliché in my old online dating profile is true: I am an animal person! I enjoy the time I spend with animals, often more than I enjoy time with people. I enjoy providing animals with a positive experience, even the ones who can be a pain in the butt. Each time I pack up from a successful stay at someone's home, I feel a strong sense of pride as I write a welcome-home note and say goodbye to their healthy and happy pets on the way out. I know I performed an invaluable service for both the client and the pets. That sense of satisfaction is what has kept me in the pet sitting industry for so many years.

Whether you are reading this as a fellow pet sitter, someone wanting to be a pet sitter, a pet owner, or someone looking for an interesting book to read, my hope is that you are entertained and also alerted to the ways in which pet sitting can go awry. In the pages that follow, I hope it will help to save you, a friend, a pet sitter, a house, or an animal or three from unnecessary trauma.

2
BLOOD, SALIVA, TEARS, AND TERROR (FOURTH OF JULY)

Whether it's Memorial Day, Labor Day, Christmas or spring break, holidays are an easy sell for any pet sitter — travel time for you? That's puppy time for me.

And yet, not all holidays are quiet, quality, creature-watching fun. In particular, the Fourth of July can be troublesome. Lucrative? Surely—lots of people travel the first week in July—but it's tremendously taxing for a pet sitter. Why is that? Look to the skies.

Those thunderously brilliant explosions lighting up the night sky, celebrating the birth of our nation? That's a red, white, and blue hell-on-Earth for dogs.

Some time ago, I was anxiously preparing for a date with a new guy named Dean, the kind who actually impressed me at a speed dating event—like finding a Ferrari at a Ford dealership. Devilishly handsome, I was enamored with him on our first date, and after some flirty email banter over a couple weeks, we agreed to get together again on the Fourth of July.

Dean reserved us a ride on the Tramway, a tram car that transports you to the top of the Sandia Mountains at the edge of Albuquerque. He got us a dinner reservation at the mountaintop restaurant and while there we planned to watch all the fireworks spanning the city vista below. In all of my years in New Mexico, I had never had the occasion to spend Independence Day that way, and my heart raced with delight. I would have to venture to the far north area of town for the date. I was in a rush to get out the door, scurrying to meet him at his place by 6 P.M., so we could arrive at the Tramway on time.

Now of course, I was pet-sitting that weekend. Holiday time is money time. I was staying at a client's home in the valley. In the house, I wrangled with two hyper Springer Spaniel sisters, Thelma and Louise. These pups would be alone for most of the evening. I was a bit queasy about having to leave them for so long, but I figured as long as I ran them wild and gave them plenty of exercise and backyard time, they'd be okay.

I fed the dogs an early dinner and made sure they got a good run around the sprawling lot for a good hour afterward. While they were playing outside, I primped for my date, carefully selecting each accessory to accent my summer dress. Makeup? On point. Sandals? Perfect. Check the mirror: dog hair. Lots of dog hair. All over me. Still...I'm ready. I'm confident. Let the fireworks begin.

Just past five, I lovingly led Thelma and Louise to their tall custom-built kennels in the garage for the night, where they had ample space to move around and stretch. I filled their water and stocked them up with chew toys. I locked up the house, left the porch light on and headed out for my midsummer's rendezvous.

I arrived at Dean's place at six sharp, and we got in his car and jutted up to the foothills to the Tramway. Dinner at the top of the mountain was extraordinary. We spent an hour or so gazing at the fireworks afterward on the outside deck, admiring the sweeping panorama. Here I was scraping the clouds and watching all the fireworks explode in magnificent bursts over the cityscape below. I suggested we head back down the Tramway to the base of the mountain because something felt off.

Even before we returned to the mountain base, I could tell that Dean was drunk, he couldn't keep his hands off of me. I urged him to wait an hour or so before driving us back to his house so I could get in my car and head home. We sat on a bench at the base of the mountain, still trying to sober up, exchanging thoughts, ideas and laughter. It was all a silly throwback to those days you'd spend in your youth, awkward butterflies, wondering who would make the next move but secretly hoping it wouldn't be you.

As it turned out, it was him. And his next move was, well...odd. He shoved his tongue into my ear.

Good God, Dean's a sloppy mess!

"What are you doing?!" I gasped, as I pulled away from him and rubbed the puddle of saliva from inside my ear with my sweater sleeve. "Yuck!"

He looked at me with wide eyes, surprised.

"I thhhhoughfft all wommmen looooove thath," he slurred. "Doesn't that turn you on?"

No, not at all.

"I don't know any women who like that, I definitely don't like it," I said, still wiping my ear and in total, unrelenting disgust.

"Oh, gee. I'm so sorry." He said with margarita breath. Defeated and unsure what else to do, he wrapped his arm around me.

After thirty minutes of pretending I was still into him, I was so, so ready to go home. It was approaching midnight, and I was done with the awkward tongue-in-ear aftermath and assorted futile attempts to arouse me and the excruciating drunken small talk. A great date that ended badly, and little did I know there was soon to be a surprise encore.

"You okay to drive?" I asked.

"Yeah," he insisted. I wasn't quite sure if he was, but sometimes you gamble with your safety to

preserve your dignity. I just wanted to get h
the dogs at that point.

We arrived at his place a short time later.
politely hugged him goodbye and left to head to my
client's home for the night. Some twenty minutes of
cautiously feathering the gas pedal later, I parked my
car in the circular driveway at my client's house.
Damn, the porch light had burnt out.

I fumbled with the key and made a myriad of
attempts to negotiate it into the lock. I could hear the
sound of eager dogs barking and squealing with
excitement from inside the garage at the other side of
the house.

Once inside the house, I headed straight to
the garage to let the dogs out of their crates and into
the backyard for a potty break. I cast open the door
and flicked on the light. What I saw was a horror
scene.

Blood spattered the concrete floor under
Thelma's chain-link crate. Thelma's blood-coated legs
and paws were a grotesque contrast to her mostly
white hair as she jumped up and down, up and down.
Chills sped up my spine. I rushed over to her and let
her out, all nervous energy as she excitedly pounced
on me, smearing her bloody paw prints all over my
dress. In that moment, I realized that the hours of
fireworks in the neighborhood had sent poor Thelma
into a frantic fight-or-flight state, and she had no
escape. I let her sister, Louise, out of her crate,
unbothered and unmoved. Nothing amiss in her crate
at all.

le business of cleaning up Thelma's —her ceramic bowl in pieces, desperate attempts to escape over er custom chain-link crate. In the have landed over and over again on the ceramic shards, which shredded her paws and the quicks of her claws. It was an awful scene. I scooped her up in my arms, carried her out back, and tossed her into the pool. Still intoxicated, I decided it was the quickest way to wash her off and to disinfect the cuts. Pool chlorine combats bacteria, so it'd be a big antibacterial bath, right? The idea seemed ingenious—plus, she liked the pool.

Once we got her rinsed off, I examined her paws under the back patio light and saw that they were not too bad. To my relief, the bleeding had subsided. Still, there was the unrated CSI episode in the garage to clean up. Broken dish, okay, that could be easily explained away, but a floor full of blood? Mercy. I had to clean it, and fast.

Anyone who's watched *CSI* knows that the quickest way to cover your tracks is to douse the concrete with bleach and let it sit there for a few minutes to do its work on the bloodstains. As the wee hours of the morning came, I soaked and scrubbed the concrete garage floor. After working till near dawn, there was no remaining trace of the events that unfolded earlier in the evening. Success.

Exhausted, I shut off the garage light and closed the door. I let the dogs out into the backyard one last time before we all had a slumber party in the guestroom.

The next afternoon I decided to check in the garage, to be sure every drop of blood had been accounted for and cleaned up. I opened the garage and noticed something that hadn't been there before: the smell of bleach. Waves upon nose-assaulting waves of bleach in the air.

The clients, due to return in three days, would return to a garage that smells like a swimming pool. Luckily, the garage was inside their property gate, so I didn't have to worry about passersby gaining access to it. I decided to leave the outer garage door open so the space could air out.

Over the next couple days, the scent of bleach subsided. By the morning of the day the owners were supposed to return, Thelma's paws looked passable, with no sign of the terror of three nights ago. I left a note about the broken bowl, saying it was knocked over in the crate and broke on the concrete. I locked up the house, drove away, and nervously waited out the anxious moments between when they'd come home and when I'd be hearing from them.

Would they smell bleach and wonder?

Would they see Thelma's healing paws?

Would their neighbors tell them that Thelma took an odd midnight dip in the pool on the Fourth of July?

One day passed. Then five days passed. Then weeks. I didn't hear from the clients. I successfully dodged that bullet and was even lucky enough to pet sit for them several more times after that.

I never saw Dean again.

3
THE HORRIBLE HELPER
AND THE LOST CAT

If there is one thing that hindered my company growth in pet sitting it was hiring. I do not like to relinquish control, especially when it involves my livelihood and professional reputation. I have often wished I could clone myself because then I'd have no doubt the job would get done right. Or if not, at least the only person I could blame would be myself.

It finally happened one August; two of my favorite clients' bookings overlapped, meaning their trips conflicted with one other. By conflicted I mean, they conflicted with me, I could not sleep in two different places at once. I would have to either turn someone down or hire help. I did not want to turn down either client and risk the possibility they'd find another sitter in the future, so I had to finally find someone to help me. A "helper," as I like to call it. It is someone helping me as an independent contractor, nothing too serious or permanent.

I thought about it for a few days and asked around a bit and no such luck. Most of my friends had their own pets or family to tend to; no one was too keen on spending a few nights in a stranger's house with unfamiliar dogs and a cat hanging around. This would be a harder sell than I thought. Just when I was about to give up on finding someone to help me, a friend of mine mentioned she had someone renting a room from her who would be perfect. "Brian is an animal lover and would probably enjoy a little getaway from the house," my friend Abby said, excited to help me.

Later that afternoon I visited Abby's house to meet Brian. He was in his late 30s, a former professor who was transitioning careers and doing a bit of travel in the process. He had moved to the area from Seattle a few months prior. He was really warm and nice (and good looking). I felt disarmed right away and felt like he could be just the helper I needed.

"I have references, if you'd like?" He asked.

"Sure, that'd be great." I nodded. He grabbed a notebook from the desk drawer near where we were standing and wrote down a few names and phone numbers of people who could vouch for his pet sitting experience. I took the list and reconfirmed the two nights I'd need him. He agreed that he was available and happy to help out. I called all of his references later that night, and they all had great things to say about Brian.

A few days later I set up a meet-and-greet with my client and Brian. I tagged along just to introduce him and be sure everything went smoothly. Everything went well, and the Siamese and two Border Collies seemed to really like Brian. The clients, Wendy and Tom, seemed to get along with him nicely too. They agreed to have him stay the first two nights and then I would stay the two nights after that, once my other stay had ended.

The next week rolled around and my other stay was coming to an end. I texted Brian to see when he would depart from Wendy and Tom's place, so I could arrive soon after to finish up the final two days of the pet sit. I arrived just before the dog's dinner time at 5 P.M. I unpacked my things, fed the pooches dinner, and settled in for the night. It dawned on me that I had not seen the cat at all yet. Their beloved Siamese cat, Stasi, was nowhere to be found. Cats can get weird and elusive when their routine is disrupted (i.e. when their owners are absent). I looked under beds, in nooks and in crannies of closets, in dark corners and behind shelves and couches. Stasi was M.I.A.

Trying not to panic just yet, I called Brian on the phone. It went to voicemail, so I left a message, "Hi Brian, this is Yvonne. I can't seem to find Stasi. I have looked all over the house and she is nowhere to be found. I am not sure when the last time you saw

her was, but if you can give me a call that'd be great."
I hung up the phone and tried to calm my nerves.

I paced around the house, double-checking everywhere I'd looked. I even checked in the garage, thinking maybe she had somehow snuck out there even though there'd be no reason Brian would have needed to be in the garage. She was not in there. I called for her over and over. I walked throughout the house shaking her crinkly bag of cat treats, but no sight of her. I could feel the panic welling up inside of me.

Then my cell phone rang. It was Brian. I nervously fumbled to answer, it as if it were a contest to answer the phone in under two seconds. I'd have won. "Hi Brian," I said, cutting to the chase. "I assume you got my message?"

"Yes, I did." He paused. "Um, I think I saw Stasi earlier today, around noon was the last time. I had the back door open for a little while and maybe she snuck out without me noticing, but I swear it wasn't open for long." He sounded too laid back for the situation at hand. I wanted to jump through the phone and choke him.

"But you are sure she was there in the morning?" I inquired, fearing the worst.

"Yes, she greeted me when I got out of the shower around nine this morning, and then I saw her eating when I returned from brunch around noon, which is the last time I definitely know I laid eyes on her," he said, sounding distracted by something.

"Well, she must have gotten out when you had the back door open because she is nowhere in the house. I've looked everywhere, rattled treats, called her, and still no sign of her," I responded, trying to keep the anger from my tone of voice. "I am going to have to call the client and see if they have any tricks for calling her," I said without waiting for his response. "I'll let you know if I find her," I finished, trying to steady my voice before hanging up. I just wanted to scream at him.

That night I was a nervous wreck, all I could think about was Stasi, and wonder where she was. I couldn't eat; I could barely breathe. The anxiety building in me felt like a slow suffocation. I frantically looked out the doors and windows every ten minutes, like a paranoid meth head. I rattled her bag of treats ceaselessly outside the front and back doors, hoping the promise of treats would entice her to appear as it usually did. Nothing.

Where was she? Terrible thoughts were swarming through my head—had she run into a coyote? I know there are coyotes heard and seen in this area. Was she trapped somewhere? Was she freezing to death in the cold winter night? Indoor cats aren't accustomed to the dropped temperatures overnight. Was she really lost, perhaps miles away by now? Would she ever find her way home?

Reluctantly, I decided I had to call Wendy and Tom to let them know what was going on. Perhaps this had happened before. Perhaps there was some sort of hiding place she liked outside. Or perhaps there was a trick of some sort to get her to come inside.

I nervously waited as the phone rang, and rang, and rang. Finally, Wendy answered.

"Hi, Yvonne, what's up?" she asked, cheerful and happy. My mouth was dry, but I forced myself to speak.

"Hi Wendy, I, I, well...Stasi got out. Brian somehow let her get out and I have had no luck finding her." I spit it out and closed my eyes tightly, as if that would make this whole nightmare go away.

"Oh, no!" Wendy said, sounding alarmed.

"I have looked outside and rattled her treat bags and called her and everything. I don't know what else to do. I am so sorry," I said, feeling a mixture of worried, mad, sad and guilty. *Damn Brian!* I thought.

Wendy was trying hard to remain calm, I could tell. I think it helped that Stasi was actually Tom's cat, so she wasn't as close to Wendy's heart as she was to Tom's, but still. This situation was probably ruining their vacation. I wanted to crawl under a rock and die.

"Take Misha for a walk around the block and she will help you look for Stasi. Call Stasi as you walk." Wendy instructed. "Misha is a smart dog, she can help you find her."

"OK, I will try that now," I said. She gave me a few more tips and we both hung up.

I was hopeful as I got Misha all harnessed and leashed up to head outside for a stroll around the block.

We walked, and walked, and walked.

I called, and called, and called.

"Stasi! Staaaasi! Stasi?" I called over and over. I yelled it. I sang it. I whistled. I shook her treat bag like maracas for an hour. Nothing. I talked to neighbors and people walking around the area and gave out my mobile number clinging to hope. No one called.

As it got dark, the temperature started to descend. We turned the corner and came to the last 100 yards of our walk to the house. I was so hopeful we'd find her that my mind actually started projecting images of her, fooling me a few times into thinking I saw her. There she is behind some bushes...well maybe not. I see her over behind that tree. I hear her meow! Over there, behind that porch swing. Nope, she wasn't there. I was officially hallucinating now. All of this worry and anticipation was making me crazy.

We arrived home and I unleashed Misha. With the adrenaline helping me as we searched for Stasi, I didn't notice how frozen my toes and fingers actually were. My fingers burned under the warm water from the sink. I defrosted them and then I gave Misha a big hug for being a good sport. We settled in for the night, but my mind was anything but settled. It was in full-on worry mode.

I somehow managed to fall asleep later that night, but only for a few minutes. I tossed and turned. At one point I got up and in my delirium of worry and unrest, I decided it'd be a good idea to leave the exterior French bedroom doors cracked a tiny bit. In case she decided to find her way home she could easily come inside. Maybe other things would come inside, too, but at this stage, it was worth the risk.

You know those moments when you are in awe of the miracles of life? When joy gushes out of your every pore? I had one of those moments about 4 A.M. the next morning.

"Mrrow. Mrrrrow. Meow." I heard a faint sound in the distance which became louder as I fully awakened.

"Stasi?" I whispered loudly as I jolted up in bed. I blinked, trying to make out the figure in the corner of the room. I couldn't tell if it was her or not, and for all I knew it could have been some stray cat announcing its arrival.

I flew out of bed and hit the light switch on the opposite side of the room. There, walking toward me, was Stasi. I was overcome with emotion! I had an ugly cry and scooped her up in my arms, so thankful she had returned in one piece. I ran to the French doors and locked them shut. My heart was beating furiously as I quickly examined her. Except for some dirt and sticks stuck to her fur, she was unscathed! I hugged and kissed her as relief relaxed my entire body. I had cared for Stasi for years and I would never forgive myself if my hired helper caused her demise.

It was 3 A.M. where my clients were vacationing in Colorado. I texted them anyway:

"Hi there, good news! Stasi just came home! I left the exterior bedroom doors cracked overnight and she just strolled in! She seems happy and fine! Just wanted to let you know! Now you can enjoy the rest of your vacation!"

I checked the text for errors and let out a huge sigh as I hit send. I collapsed on the bed overjoyed. Losing a pet, whether it is yours or someone else's, is the worst feeling in the world.

I didn't bother to inform Brian that I had found Stasi. This would be the first and last time I'd ever use him to help with my client's care. I was so pissed at him for the past twelve hours of hell that I had to endure, not to mention my clients. That, and he seemed so lackadaisical about the whole thing. In pet sitting you can be a lot of things, but careless is not one of them.

I would have expected to lose Wendy and Tom as clients after this ordeal, but luckily they knew it was not my fault. They were so gracious and kind about the whole incident. We continued to have a great working relationship for many years to come.

4
LOST AND FOUND, AND KEPT

An acquaintance of mine asked me if it was OK to give my information to a friend of hers who was in need of a pet sitter. This was back in the early days and she knew I was looking for clients. She referred me to a girl she'd known for many years, I'll call her Becky. Becky lived in Canada but it was her father who lived nearby who would need my services.

I agreed to meet up with Rich and his adult daughter, Becky, who was in town for a few days before returning to Canada where her father would join her for his vacation. I communicated with Becky via email, and we agreed to meet on a Wednesday night at the house. He lived a few miles away from me in a trailer park in a sketchy part of town. I suppose the part of town was OK, but it was the rundown trailer park that made it seem sketchy.

I arrived on time and parked on the street. This would be a first, as I had never stayed in a trailer before. I didn't want to buy into the "trailer trash" stereotypes. I reminded myself that it was the dogs I was there for, not the amenities. I figured it'd be a good experience to get under my belt, no matter what. Later I'd discover what a severely underestimated assumption that'd be.

The trailer park was what you'd expect—lots of cars on the street with many shabby properties. Junk cars parked on lawns, falling fences, overgrown weeds and non-existent landscaping. I walked up to the house on the crackling old deck, which looked like it would crumble under the slightest weight. I knocked on the door and an eruption of high-pitched doggie barking ensued. I could hear them quieting the dogs as they approached the door.

Becky opened the door with one dog in her arms, "Hi, I'm Becky" she said and stood to the side so I could enter. She seemed to be in her late 30s, tall and blonde. "Did you find it OK?" she asked. I replied, "Yes, you gave great directions. I found it just fine." Both dogs started to quiet down a bit and began sniffing my ankles vigorously. They appeared to be Pekinese: small, brown, bulging eyes and lively. I pet the male who had propped his front legs up on my calf. He seemed happy to greet me all the while curiously sniffing away.

I took a seat on the couch where Rich was also seated. He looked to be in his late-60s with bushy eyebrows and a head of gray hair. Becky sat down and let the dog she had in her arms go. The little dog ran directly to me. "That is Mindy," Becky said sweetly, smiling as Mindy propped her front paws up on my knees. "That's Mork, he can be a little skittish but he's a lover," she warned. Mork was furiously sniffing my sneakers while keeping a cautious eye on me. As I patted his little head, he paused for a minute and looked up at me.

"So I'm going to stay with my daughter Becky up in Canada for a couple of weeks next month, and so we'll need someone to stay with the dogs for that entire time. You stay overnights, is that right?" Rich asked and looked over at me with an unsure, hopeful look on his face.

"Yes, I stay overnights," I said looking at him while petting Mindy who was now in my lap trying to lick my face. I turned away for a brief second to dodge the wet dog tongue darting at my face. "I specialize in overnights because it is easiest for me and the pets are happier that way."

"Great, that is just what we need," Becky nodded, amid approving sentiments from her father. There was a more welcoming feeling in the room, and we started to chit-chat a bit.

I asked some preliminary questions: Are the dogs healthy? Recent or chronic illnesses? Any behavior quirks or special needs? Luckily, both Mork and Mindy seemed to be healthy and happy little dogs. I learned that they were originally Rich's wife's dogs, but she had passed away about a year prior. It was clear he had taken over their care, despite being somewhat indifferent to them. After chatting for a few minutes, I got a strong feeling that the dogs' needs and routines were something of a burden to him, which was odd for a pet owner. Maybe the dogs reminded him too much of his late wife, and he just wanted to close that chapter.

With all of the initial discussion out of the way, they gave me a brief tour of the trailer. It was not large—it had two bedrooms: a master and a smaller bedroom. It had two bathrooms, a kitchen, and a laundry closet. The yard was what you'd expect to find in a trailer park – a small chain-link fenced area around the back and side of the trailer. A small yard even for small Mork and Mindy, but at least it was a yard!

I was taken aback when Rich showed me a pistol hidden under some hand towels on top of the dresser in the master bedroom. "Now, don't be afraid to use this. It's here for your protection," he said nonchalantly. He saw the alarm on my face and backpedaled, trying to downplay the fact that he was showing me a loaded gun and giving me permission to use it! "Nothing strange has ever happened here but you just never know. It is better to be safe than sorry." He added. *You're showing me a pistol within ten minutes of meeting me and nothing strange has ever happened here? Somehow, I doubt that.* I thought. The last thing I wanted to do was to have to shoot and potentially kill someone. Now I was really wondering what happened to his wife.

These people were a bit unrefined, it occurred to me. Something seemed off, but I wasn't sure what exactly it was. They confirmed the price per night, which was a modest $28, and paid me via a Canadian check for the 13 nights. I finished writing my notes, gave them my business card, and got up and left.

A couple weeks later, I returned to the house to begin my stay there. I did not feel comfortable; there was something about that gun in the master bedroom that stayed on my mind. *Please don't let me have to use it*, I thought as I unpacked my clothes. I set down my bag eyeing the folded hand towels covering the gun on the dresser. I felt uneasy.

After I unpacked my food and clothes, I let Mork and Mindy out in the yard to do their business. It was early December and cold and they hesitated to go out but they eventually got their business done in the yard. I tried to focus on the good thing about this stay: the animals are grateful. They greeted me with the best happy-dog tail wagging, and I felt welcomed immediately. I think they must have missed having a female human in the house. In my experience, many dogs are partial to women over men.

The first few nights I slept well. The bed wasn't particularly comfortable, but it was a king size so there was plenty of space for me to find a spot that worked. The dogs slept on the other end of the bed. One of them threw up on the second night. I left a voicemail for the owners because I wasn't sure what to clean the spot with, there was no detergent anywhere in the house. It was little things like this that were unusual. No detergent. No iron. No heat?

I returned from some errands on my fourth morning there and the house was ice cold. It was fifty degrees outside and maybe sixty-two degrees in the house at that point. The dogs were huddled together on the couch. I took off the heater cover and examined it, everything looked as though it should be working. After thirty minutes, I gave up and called their "emergency" contact, which was Rich's brother Stan who lived across town.

Stan's voicemail picked up after several rings so I left a message. A couple hours later and no call from Stan, I tried him and Rich again. Both calls went to voicemail. I was getting frustrated. There was a snow storm coming in that night and I knew I needed to do something before the roads got bad. Just as I was about to check my weather app, my phone rang. It was my helper, who was doing overnights uptown for another client of mine.

"Hi Yvonne, this is Tanya. I hate to say this but I am completely snowed in. I am not going to be able to make it down into uptown, my car is stuck about two hundred yards from my house," She said sounding as if she had just climbed a mountain. *Shit.* "It has been snowing real bad this side of the mountain and I drove up here this afternoon to take care of some things here at my home and before I knew it the snow had multiplied and driving out just now, my car got stuck."

"Are you sure there is no way you can make it down?" I asked before realizing that this could be a good solution for my dilemma. I could take Mork and Mindy down to the uptown house for the night while the heater issue got resolved.

"No, we have been trying to dig out for almost an hour, I'm afraid unless some snow melts, my car will be stuck in there for a while," she said, sounding hopeless.

"OK, I'll head to uptown for the night and take care of them. What is the garage entry code?" I asked, digging in my purse for a pen.

"It is 4205, and sometimes you have to hit enter twice, it is a little testy," Tanya said sounding relieved to have me take over her scheduled pet sit for the night. "Luckily, I left their dog care instructions on the counter inside the house. You'll find that everything is pretty straightforward." She said.

"Thanks, I will head down to uptown shortly. I will touch base with you tomorrow to see if you're able to dig out of the snow." I said and hung up. Tanya was usually a good helper, but unfortunately, she lived out in the boonies where it snowed much more than in the city.

Meanwhile, back at the trailer, I texted the owner and his brother, and again I received no response. These people were definitely of a different breed, I decided. Most clients pay good attention to their phone while on vacation, and especially if the pet sitter calls. Never in my career had I experienced several hours without a return call or text message from a client on vacation.

I packed Mork and Mindy up in my car along with their dog beds and food and we headed south about five miles to the house uptown. By the time we arrived at the house it was sleeting heavily, but wasn't sticking to the ground yet so the roads were just wet.

On my way over I got a call from Stan, Rich and Becky's "emergency contact". Unfortunately, Stan had been drinking and was too inebriated to understand the gravity of the situation. "There is no heat in the trailer and it is freezing cold. I have tried to fix it but I can't figure it out. Rich, your brother, left your information for me to call in case of an emergency. This is an emergency." I repeated it slowly and loudly over and over, with no sign of comprehension on his part.

I was pissed. Not only were Rich and Becky in another country and not answering their phones, they provided an emergency contact who was useless as well. After a while, I just gave up and hung up the phone on Stan. I tried him the next afternoon, and he had no recollection of our conversation; he also failed to understand the urgency of having no heat in mid-December. (Gold star for Stan for being the worst emergency contact ever.)

I arrived at the house shortly after I hung up on Stan. I entered using the garage code that Tanya gave me, no problem. I introduced Mork and Mindy to Gary, the old dog at the uptown house. He growled and seemed rather displeased that two little dogs had invaded his home. I couldn't blame him because I knew it was not good to bring another client's dogs to a home where the client wasn't present, nor did they give permission. I had no other choice, Tanya was unable to get her car unstuck and I had to get Mork and Mindy out of that freezing trailer. And who knows when the heater would get fixed? We'd probably freeze to death before I ever saw Stan.

In my mind, I justified the situation as the only viable option. I had to keep the dogs separated because Gary was so upset they were on his turf. I closed off Mork and Mindy in the back laundry room which had a doggie door to the backyard attached. I figured they'd be safe in there, separated from Gary.

I had dinner plans with a friend about an hour later so I made sure all the dogs were comfortable and had fresh water before I left.

A couple hours later, I returned. Luckily the sleeting snow still wasn't sticking, so the roads were drivable. I came in through the garage door, Gary was sleeping soundly at the foot of the couch. He stirred awake and stretched as my boot heels clunked on the hardwood floor. I felt guilty as I headed to the laundry room to check on Mork and Mindy.

Mork and Mindy were nowhere to be found. The laundry room was empty. I opened the back door and called for them outside and they never came. I grabbed the flashlight near the back door and looked in every nook and cranny of the backyard while hollering their names. Nothing. No sign of Mork or

Mindy. I walked around the side of the house to check the gate and it was then I realized they must have escaped through the rungs in the iron gate, the gaps in which were big enough for the little dogs to squeeze through.

My mind would not let me believe that they actually got out of the gate. How on earth would they get out? They had no interest in the outdoors before, no interest in the snow or cold before, why on earth would they venture out in the sleeting, cold and dark night? I went back inside the back door and rechecked the laundry room in disbelief looking in every tiny space, just in case. A sharp ache of regret, guilt and panic drove through my stomach up to my chest.

I jumped in my car and drove circles around the neighborhood for hours, and then on foot for an hour with a flashlight. I yelled out "Mork and Mindy" until my throat went hoarse. Feeling hopeless and exhausted I returned to the client's house. Around midnight I finally retreated to bed. I didn't sleep a wink that night.

The next morning at first light I got up and posted on Craigslist. Their lost pets community forum was a long-shot but it was at least still a shot. I took it. I then went to work on my laptop creating "LOST" flyers with photos of the dogs on it. I was lucky to have some good photos of them that I had taken earlier in the week when I sent some photos to their owners. Luckily there was a copy shop right around the corner. I had black and white flyers I made printed up on standard sheets of paper. I bought a roll of clear packing tape while I was there.

Later that morning I canvassed the neighborhood with the "LOST" flyers and posted them on every pole, bench, and stop-sign within a 2-mile radius. I felt like a zombie on a mission. I'd gotten no sleep and the impending doom was that the dogs were hurt, dead, or that they'd never be found at all. All three scenarios danced in my head causing my stomach to burn and my head to ache simultaneously. *Maybe I could get lost too, and then I wouldn't have to deal with this whole nightmare.*

All that day and the next I was a mess. I could barely eat or sleep. I imagined Rich shooting me with that gun. My friends and family, and the public would know me to be a terrible pet sitter, never mind the backstory. I'd be condemned in the pet sitting community, never to pet sit again. I woke up in a cold sweat the next night—I think the five minutes I'd actually slept I must've had a terrible dream about the whole thing.

I thought the ordeal had come to an end two days later when I got a text from a woman who said she had found the dogs. I was beside myself with excitement. I wolfed down a whole frozen pizza that day waiting for her to return my call. I could breathe again and my appetite had returned! If there is one thing good about trauma, it is weight loss. I call it the life-went-to-shit diet and in my experience, it is quite effective. You know you're in deep when weight loss due to starvation is the only silver lining of a situation.

"Hello, this is Yvonne," I answered when the woman finally returned my call an hour later.

"Hi, this is Roberta. I think I have your two dogs, I saw a sign in my neighborhood." She said, sounding a bit timid.

"Great! Are they OK?" I asked.

"Yes, they are well, I found them walking in the dark on Friday night around 7 P.M.," she said. "Are they your dogs?" she asked directly.

"I am so glad they are ok! No, they aren't my dogs, I am pet sitting for a client in your area," I said, feeling my entire body relax.

"Well, how would I know you have permission to have the dogs?" She asked quickly in a questioning tone.

"I have the client's key, you can call them and ask them. I can give you their number." A burst of butterflies was fluttering in my stomach. Roberta couldn't actually be questioning my legitimacy, could she? Why on earth would I go through the trouble of posting all those missing signs in the freezing cold weather if I wasn't responsible for the dogs? I must have missed a memo from crazy somewhere.

"Well unless you have an agreement of some sort, I am not sure I can give you the dogs...I mean, how do I know you are actually the caretaker?" she asked seriously. I almost choked as the air got sucked out of my lungs. Was I hearing this woman correctly?

"You can copy my ID, I have photos of the dogs on my camera. "I will gladly give you the owner's contact information," I rambled in a flurry. "Please, I promise I am responsible for them."

"Sure, yes. Give me the owner's contact information," She instructed coldly.

Was this really happening? I thought. I had finally found the dogs and this crazy woman was demanding that I prove my worthiness? Unbelievable.

"OK, hang on, let me look up the number," I said as I scrolled through my phone's contacts list to find Rich and Becky's numbers, I scribbled them down on the back of an envelope which was lying on the counter beside me. I got back on the line and gave Roberta their numbers.

"You'll probably want to leave a voicemail if you don't get an answer," I said. "They're in Canada, and I haven't had the best luck getting in touch with them." I said hoping she'd realize that I was genuine.

"Well, I will have to make sure and I'll get back to you," she said and hung up the phone.

I was stunned and threw down my phone on the couch. The tears came quick and poured down my cheeks. I felt helpless. This woman, Roberta, clearly either had trust issues or was some sort of moron. I didn't know what to think but I knew something wasn't right, something in her tone. My gut told me this was going to be a battle.

Later that night, after hours of desperate thoughts, it occurred to me to look up Roberta's phone number online. In Google I typed in the first three digits, space, then the next three, space, then the last four and I hit enter. I held my breath. The search results displayed a legal website, and I clicked on the listing and did a search on the website page for her phone number digits. "Roberta Snell" was the name that showed up next to her mobile phone number. BINGO.

I felt a small sense of reassurance knowing that at least I had Roberta's last name, place of work, and mobile phone number confirmed. I wasn't sure what to do with all of that information yet, but at least I had it if I needed to use it.

I called the client Rich and his daughter Becky in Canada and let them know of the situation. Unfortunately, they both still were not answering their phones so both calls went straight to voicemail:

"Hi this is Yvonne, and I am not sure if you've gotten my voicemails about your heater not working but I had to transport the dogs to a different location so we wouldn't freeze and they got loose out a backyard gate. Luckily, they were found in the neighborhood unhurt. The woman who found them is Roberta, and she will be calling you to verify that I am allowed to have the dogs back. I just wanted to give you a heads up that she'll be calling you soon."

I hung up wondering if they had gotten any of the messages up to this point. It was so odd that I had left so many messages about their heater days ago and no response. If there was a "terrible clients" list they would top it. Apparently, a trip to Canada meant dropping off the face of the planet. The situation was maddening.

I had restless sleep that night. The next afternoon I called Roberta, having not heard from her 24 hours. Thankfully, she answered.

"Hi Roberta, this is Yvonne. I am calling about the dogs. Did you have a chance to talk to the owners yet? I haven't been able to get ahold of them." I said.

"No, I haven't been able to reach them either," she said. "The dogs are doing really well, but I am sorry I am not going to be able to give them up until I hear from the owners." She said in a cold tone.

I had been hopeful, but another part of me was expecting the answer she gave me. And from her stern and paranoid tone, I wasn't even sure that she'd give me the dogs if she did, in fact, get ahold of the owners. I was starting to realize that Roberta was a little "off".

"Hopefully we hear from them soon." I said, feeling like screaming at her. Back at square one, I hung up the phone. Roberta wasn't going to budge.

Within the next week, I managed to find out Roberta's home address by putting in her first and last name into the County's property search database online. There popped up her address along with her husband's name, Jorge. I searched the street address online and a map popped up. Sure enough, her home address was within a half-mile of where Mork and Mindy escaped from at my other client's place in the uptown area. There was no doubt I had the correct Roberta Snell and the correct address.

The next day I drove by her house just to see what it looked like. The day after that I took Gary for a walk past the house. I was so tempted to peek in but her neighbor was doing yard work outside and I didn't want to bring attention to myself.

A few more days passed. I drove by it again and I got up the nerve to approach the house. I found myself standing on Roberta's front doorstep hearing Mork and Mindy barking on the other side of the door. I knew it was them because they had distinct high-pitched, raspy barking. I rang the doorbell several times. No answer. Standing there, I called Becky and I called Rich, explaining that I had tracked the dog's location down.

Of course, neither one answered their phones or returned my calls.

As I hung up the phone, I stared at it wishing for someone to return my call. It slowly occurred to me that perhaps the only person who cared about returning the dogs to Rich was me. It wasn't Roberta, it wasn't Becky, and it wasn't Rich. Nearly a week had passed and I was the only one concerned. I was the only one trying to take any action. It was clear to me that Roberta wanted those dogs, and probably had a conversation with Rich. Rich simply surrendered his dogs to her without Becky and me knowing, quite possibly.

In that moment I decided to let it be. I had spent days stressing about the situation that no one else seemed to care much about. I walked down the driveway with a weird sense of relief at this realization. As it turned out, I wouldn't hear from someone until a month later when Rich finally returned to town and contacted me to return the trailer keys. I dropped them off when he wasn't there, I hid them in a planter in his backyard.

Many years later now, in retrospect, I have to believe that Rich decided to simply let Roberta have Mork and Mindy. As luck would have it, Roberta was in the right place at the right time when she spotted those dogs wandering the streets that night. Rich didn't care enough to ensure there was heat on in his trailer. He didn't return calls or voicemails, he simply did not care.

In a weird way, I felt like the victim in all of this. The dogs went to a seemingly better home, Rich got to frolic around in Canada indefinitely with his daughter Becky, and I had nightmares about the whole thing for weeks. I was glad that gun didn't play more of a role in this story but I should have seen it as the red-flag that it was and stayed far away from those people.

After this fiasco, I learned the hard way, to always require a signed agreement granting me access to the home and to the pets. I also learned never to accept foreign checks. Yes, Rich's daughter Becky had paid me with a bad Canadian check. Are you surprised? I am not.

5
A KILLER NEXT DOOR

It was a Tuesday evening and I slowly rolled up on the street, careful to not hit the curb while simultaneously squinting to see if the house number was correct. 113. Yes, I had arrived. There was an old truck parked under the big tree right in front of the house, so I parked just before the driveway in front of the house next door. I rolled to a stop and put my car in park. I took my own little dog, Jiminey Cricket, out of his car-seat, leashed him and set him down on the street. I gathered my clipboard and purse, shut the door, and walked up the driveway to the front door.

This couple had found me by searching on the New Mexico Pet Sitters' Alliance website; I had been getting a lot of inquiries for business via the website. It was really growing my business. I knew from our email correspondence that they were planning to go on a 3-week vacation to a remote village in the Abruzzo Mountains outside of Rome. Mary and Dan Bergh were an older artsy couple who lived near the University. Judging from their initial detailed email, they seemed like an interesting couple.

The neighborhood was what one would call a university jungle—lots of small, older homes with lots of cars on the streets. Cozy places with a few newer homes sprinkled throughout. Charming, really. Well, mostly. This wasn't one of the best-kept homes. It was shabby out front, with chipping paint and overgrown ivy and grass. It had lots of character. I could tell before knocking that the people inside would be laidback.

The owner, Mary, opened the door and greeted me with her husband, Dan, next to her. They smiled and stepped back so I could enter. The home was just what I would have imagined when looking at the outside—lots of character in the varied, old furniture. Some adorning wear and tear, mismatched colors and real, old wood. It had a very homey feel to it. I liked it. In one room, off to the side of the main living room, I could see books filling shelves floor to ceiling. I would later learn that Dan worked at the library and was an avid reader of literature. The books in the library room were his collection, his favorites.

The usual introductions happened, along with the usual questions from clients: How long have you been pet sitting? Why? How much do you charge, again? And my usual questions to clients: Where are you traveling to? Have you ever used a pet sitter before? How old are your pets?

Any recent or chronic illnesses?

Yes, there were. Ana, their elderly cat, had to have insulin shots twice a day, twelve hours apart. It wasn't an ideal situation, but it certainly wasn't terrible. I had never given a cat shots before, but I was about to learn. They had saved her shot for me to give right then, to be sure we both felt comfortable. If there is one thing you don't want, it is to be out of the country while your bitchy cat combats the squeamish pet sitter as she tries in vain to administer said shot.

Mary was delighted to inform me that Ana didn't fight the shots and she was good about taking them. She was a 16-year-old orange mixed-breed cat. Ana sat there and stared at me, daring me to come near her. Jiminey was a hyper mess. He was hyperventilating at the sight of two cats within his pouncing distance. Lucy ran to hide, but Ana stood there like a bad ass, just glaring at him. Jiminey could hardly contain his excitement. Panting and eager to chase, he bounced over to her and she shriveled up her cat nose and hissed at him coldly warning him to stay put. One reason I loved my dog was because he too, was a bad ass. He didn't care who you were, a bitchy cat or a Pitbull, he would approach and boldly ask, "What's up?" I wish I were more like my dog.

Unfortunately, being Jiminey was not good for Jiminey that day. In a split second, Ana swiftly reached out and clawed at Jiminey and sliced his tongue. She could have easily sliced it in half, but luckily, she did not. Just a couple millimeters were cut in the side. It left Jiminey lapping up blood and flicking little specks of blood everywhere. He didn't know what to do. I didn't know what to do, but I was not amused. Seeing my beloved dog hurt and bleeding was too much for me. It took everything I had to play it cool and not just dart out of there.

Mary and Dan were unfazed. They offered up a Kleenex and I wiped Jiminey's tongue, which kept bleeding while they ignored it and kept talking. I held him in my arms after that. I didn't trust Ana, and Jiminey would have gladly approached her again. While Ana continued to glare at Jiminey and me, I continued to talk to Dan and Mary about the duties involved in the pet sit. The extensive hand-watering in front and back. The special food I was to leave out for the stray cats in the front and back yards. The reasons why their college-aged son, who lived in the area, could not be bothered to lift a finger while they were gone away. Blah-blah-blah. They went on and on. By the end of the visit, I had a blood-soaked tissue and no interest in taking the job.

When it was time to go, I carried Jiminey in my arms and hurried out to my car. "I'll be in touch!" I said, waving as I unlocked my car door and got in.

A few days later, my instincts were still screaming at me to bail on this gig. I sent Mary and Dan an email explaining that I didn't think I would be the right person for the job. I wanted my Jiminey to be happy, and I didn't want Ana to feel threatened or unhappy. I really wanted to tell them the truth – that I just felt a bad vibe all around. Everything just felt wrong from their bitchy cats to their unconcern for my dog, to their required thirty minute daily hand-watering, to their weirdly unhelpful son just a few miles away. I knew in my gut that if I stayed there something bad would happen, I could feel it.

I could sense the disappointment in Mary and Dan's response. Their words were complimentary and encouraging because they still wanted me to stay there and do the job despite my initial fears.

"Remember, Ana is an indoor/outdoor cat, and if you feel uncomfortable just leave her outside. She knows when to come around for her insulin shots, so it should be no problem. Really, please reconsider," Mary's email pleaded.

I felt bad. I knew that I was probably the only hope for these two to get a pet sitter. They had a month left until their trip and I suspected they were running out of options. Three weeks is a long time to do overnights, and many pet sitters aren't keen on long stays like this would be. I knew they had interviewed a few pet sitters already, but for whatever reason decided not to use them. Or maybe the pet sitters felt what I felt too, and bailed.

Before responding I decided to sleep on it and respond the next morning. I was still torn the next morning, but decided it was unprofessional to make them wait any longer for a confirmation. I emailed:

"Hi Dan and Mary, I wanted to let you know that I gave this a lot of thought and I will go ahead and do the pet sit for you. I am very concerned about my Jiminey getting along with your cat Ana, but I will separate them if I have to. Please let me know when I can come get your house key within the next couple of weeks before you leave on your trip. Thanks, Yvonne"

I hit send and felt a bit of relief, mainly for them. Not for me. I had a sinking feeling in my stomach, which I ignored the next few weeks until the pet sit there started. I was dreading it but couldn't quite pinpoint why. It was probably because my intuition sensed that every pet sitter's worst nightmare was about to come true.

I'd picked up the key and paperwork a few days before they left on their trip, and arrived on a Thursday evening with my bag of food, clothes, and toiletries. I unloaded my car, including Jiminey Cricket. He bounced merrily up to the door. I was less than thrilled but was trying to make the best of it. Ana was already outside, so I knew it would be ok to leave Jiminey inside the house while I unpacked my car.

I had just unloaded the last of my bags and was headed down the driveway to close my trunk when the neighbor across the street hurried toward me.

"Hi, you must be their pet sitter?" She smiled, stepping up on the sidewalk.

"Yes, I'm Yvonne," I said and held out my hand to shake hers.

"I just wanted you to know that if you need anything at *all* I am right across the street. I work from home as a massage therapist. My name is Nova," she said, clutching my arm in a motherly fashion. She leaned in as if to reveal a secret, "Oh, and these people pretend to care for their pets but they don't! They are left outside all the time and their grown son doesn't care either. Last time he was supposed to stop by and, you know, I didn't see his car parked there *once* the whole week that they were gone! I am so glad they finally got serious and hired someone!" She clearly had a lot to get off her chest.

My mouth hung open. Was this a nosy neighbor, or a genuine one? I got a feeling it was a mixture of both. I decided to be honest with her.

"You know, my instincts were telling me something was off about this place and these people!" I said, feeling a wave of relief that I wasn't imagining it all. "When I came over for the meet-and-greet a few weeks ago, their cat sliced my little dog's tongue with her claw. They didn't seem to care much, if at all. We were lucky he didn't need stitches!" I said. "I tried to turn them down with a nice email, but they talked me into it." I felt like hugging her and sobbing at the same time. If this neighbor ran over to immediately console and warn me now, what the hell was in store for me later?

"Oh honey, I am so sorry that happened to your little dog. That cat is old and not friendly." Nova said. "They had another cat who ran away last year." She informed me. "These people are just not right," Nova warned. "Here is my card. Really, if you need anything at all, call me!"

"Here, let me get you my card too," I said, and opened my car to get to the stack of business cards I had in my center console. "Here you go."

We talked for a few minutes more and she dashed back across the street to her house. It was dusk now and the temperature had dropped. I walked back to the house and settled in for the night. I unpacked my things: fridge and freezer foods first, then pantry items, then toiletries and clothes. I was ready for my three-week stay.

Little did I know how truly *not ready* I was.

A few days passed and things were going all right. I was managing to give Ana her insulin shots twice daily without incident. Both Ana and Lucy ate well and seemed happy and healthy. The stray cats outside were eating from the bowls regularly, too. Routines were in motion.

I had not seen Ana in nearly a day. It was the fifth night and I called and called for Ana, I yelled at the top of my lungs. I am sure the entire neighborhood was tired of my incessant yelling but I had to administer her insulin shot! Where was she? I gave up after about thirty minutes of yelling in the front and backyard. I'd open the doors every hour or so, but there was no sight of her. It was near midnight so I headed for bed.

The next morning, I called again for Ana, but there was still no sign of her. Lucy hung around the back porch and would lounge on the wicker chair in the sun for half the day, but Ana was nowhere to be found. I hoped for the best and headed out for work that morning.

After lunch, I saw a voicemail notification on my phone. I listened to the message and found it was Nova, the neighbor I had met from across the street. Her voice was high pitched like she was crying. *Wait, she* is *crying*, I realized, and plugged my other ear so I could hear the recording more clearly.

"I heard you calling for Ana outside this morning and I just found her. The Jack Russell Terrier next door escaped yesterday and he must have got ahold her because I just found her in the neighbor's yard!" she cried. "That Jack Russell really hates cats and he chased her before some months back," she rambled. "Oh, it looked like it was a struggle. Oh, poor Ana. She was completely stiff and cold when I found her in the neighbor's yard. I have placed her in a box and I set it in the bed of the old truck in front of where you're staying." She sounded extremely upset. "I am so sorry Yvonne. Please call me."

She left her number and hung up.

I set my phone down on my desk. My heart felt like a rock, I could actually feel my chest tighten with anxiety. Holy shit! My client's cat had died, on my watch. This was a first, and every pet sitter's absolute worst nightmare. I could feel the tears welling up in my eyes. I tried to ignore my coworker's laughter as I got up to escape to the restroom to bawl my eyes out.

"Hey, Yvonne, check out this email my friend just forwarded to me, it is hilariou—Yvonne? What's wrong?" My coworker, Lana, intercepting me, noticed the tears welling in my eyes. I tried to hide but it was too late.

"I couldn't find my client's cat last night or this morning. I just got a voicemail. Their neighbor called and said she found the cat dead in a neighbor's yard after apparently having a brawl with another neighbor's dog that got loose yesterday." I rubbed my forehead. "Oh my God. I don't know what to do! The clients don't return for another two weeks. What am I going to do about their cat?" I felt sick hearing myself say it all aloud.

Lana hugged me and tried to console me.

"Oh, it's not your fault. These things happen." She said, rubbing my back.

Actually, they don't happen. Pets might die under the care of other sitters, but never under my care! She was not helping me feel better.

"What am I supposed to do with a dead cat for two weeks?" I asked, visualizing a maggot-filled rotting cat sitting in the truck bed for the next two weeks. Pure horror.

"Freeze it," Lana said calmly. "You can take it to their veterinarian and they most likely have huge freezers and they'll freeze it for you, I bet! I know because my sister used to work at a vet's office." She said, assuring me.

"Really?" I looked up at her, grabbing a tissue to dry my eyes. "They'll freeze a dead cat for two weeks?" I asked in disbelief. She nodded in agreement.

In a daze, I left work early that day and headed to the client's place to get the cat out of the bed of the truck. I called Nova on the way there and we both had a good cry. I don't know which was worse: actually finding the dead cat and boxing it up, or being responsible for it and having to inform its owners that it had died.

Officially, Nova and I were both having the worst week ever.

"What are you going to do with Ana?" Nova asked me after a few minutes on the phone. By that point, I tried not to think of her as Ana. I was too emotional. I had to think of her as the cat. Even though she was bitchy, she was still someone's pet and I felt horrible.

"I am taking her to her veterinarian's office. I called earlier and they agreed to freeze her there until the Berghs get back from their trip." I said.

"Oh, thank gosh!" Nova said. "I'm so glad."

"I am, too. I tried to get ahold of their son, but he was a complete jerk. He didn't seem to care one ounce. This way at least they can decide what to do with her when they return." I felt simultaneous relief and terror as I said that.

When they return, God! When they return they'll have to bury their cat. I felt sick again at the thought.

I ended the conversation, and a few minutes later I arrived at the house. There in the bed of the truck was an old boot box with a furry orange leg protruding from it. I felt a wave of sadness come over me as I looked at the box and touched the leg. It was stiff and cold. It was really true. Ana was dead. I couldn't bear to open the box. I didn't want to be further traumatized by a mangled dead cat staring back at me.

I put it in my trunk and drove to the veterinarian's office a few miles away.

"Hi," I greeted the receptionist, "I called earlier. I have the Bergh's cat Ana in my trunk." I said lowering my voice so the customers in the waiting area wouldn't overhear.

"Oh, yes. Hi. I am so sorry. Let me help you with that," she said warmly and walked around the side of the desk. She followed me outside to the parking lot. "Did you tell the Bergh's?" She asked.

"No, I still can't get ahold of them," I explained. "They are in a remote village in the Abruzzo mountains outside of Rome. I left a message at the front desk, but the lady said they don't have phones in the rooms and the cabins are not attached to the main building where the front desk is."

"I hate to say this," she said, "but I used to pet sit all the time and the worst shit would happen when people would leave the country. Like it was a curse or something. All the forces of nature conspire once clients leave the country. It got so bad that I started to say no to client's planning to leave the country on vacation. Like, sorry, you'll need to find someone else, I'm not your sitter," she said and laughed a little, trying to lighten the mood and make me feel better. I wasn't quite sure it was helping but I was glad that I wasn't alone in the shit show that was my life at that moment.

"Here she is," I said as I opened my trunk and peered down at the stiff cat leg sticking out from the box.

"Oh. Poor baby!" she said, trying to sound warm, but it came out cold. I figured she was probably way too used to this kind of thing. She slowly lifted the box out of the trunk and I closed it shut.

"Thank you. I will put a note in the system to call them around the 26th to come get her." She said as she walked up the stairs toward the building.

"Thank you, I'll leave them a note too!" I said nodding to her as she pushed open the front door with her back and disappeared inside.

I left and drove straight to the grocery store for a bottle of Cabernet. As if wine were a way to bring cats back to life, I downed the whole bottle later that night while watching mindless reality shows. While I zoned out trying to forget the day's events, Jiminey seemed restless. Surely he could sense that something was amiss with me.

The next day I phoned the village again. The woman who answered insisted she would relay to the Berghs to call me as soon as possible. I had told her about the situation with Ana, which was probably a good thing because the woman chose not to tell the Berghs to call me until their last week there. I got a call about six-thirty in the morning two days before the end of my stay at their house. Dan was on the other end of the line.

"Hi, Yvonne. We just got a message from the desk to phone you," he said through the poor line connection.

"Yes, I have to tell you that something has happened to Ana," I cut to the chase, not knowing how long or good the phone connection would be. "I am so sorry to have to tell you this but your neighbor's dog got loose and chased her and got her. She succumbed to her injuries and your neighbor Nova found her dead in another neighbor's yard," I blurted out nervously.

I never imagined I'd be telling someone their loved one, a human, nor furry, had died. It was an awful moment.

He paused and sighed.

"Oh, I am so sorry that happened while you were there," he said slowly. "Oh, that is too bad. Oh, poor Ana." His voice cracked. I knew he was choking back his emotions. Despite Nova's negative opinion of them, I figured they probably really cared for Ana to endure the expense of insulin shots, and now I knew it without a doubt. I felt so horrible bearing the bad news, I wanted to disappear.

"I've placed her at your veterinarian's office. They were happy to freeze her until you return. I know that sounds bad, but they assured me it happens on occasion," I explained, trying to reassure him.

"That is just fine. Again, I am so sorry this happened during your stay," he said, sounding melancholy.

"I feel so bad," I told him. "Lucy and your gardens are all doing just fine. Everything else is going very smoothly." I desperately tried to sound upbeat.

A couple of days later, when my stay came to an end, I prepared a nice sympathy card I had purchased after Ana died. I left it on the counter with the welcome-home note I typically write to all of my clients. A card was the least I could do in this horrible situation.

When the Berghs returned to town, they sent me an email thanking me for everything and apologizing for the events that unfolded. I think they must have felt some responsibility because they had ultimately talked me into doing the pet sit after I had tried to turn them down. I felt some solace in that, but the fact that their beloved cat died on my watch was still troubling.

They weren't frequent travelers so just over a year later they called me to pet sit for them again. I promptly and politely turned them down. I lied claiming I had another obligation. I didn't want to go near that house or those people ever again. When a cat nearly slices off your dog's tongue with a swift swipe of its claw, it is a clear message to stay away.

6
PET SITTING FOR A LOCAL CELEBRITY

Celebrities have pets and need pet care, too. Yes, it is true. The truth is, celebrities are just like any other client, but they tend to be a bit more particular, as you might expect. Believe it or not, I feel more confident knowing a new client, or celebrity, conducts a thorough screening prior to hiring me. It is a little ego boost knowing I passed the test!

An acquaintance of mine, Kristen, who was well connected in town, mentioned that she had recently lunched with Cindy, one of the nightly news anchors in town. Cindy needed to find a reliable pet sitter to stay at her place with her pets while she went on a few upcoming trips.

Kristen, as it turns out, thought of me. "Would you be interested in pet sitting for her? I believe she has a Rottweiler and a cat."

"Sure. Why not? Do you know if the Rott is friendly?" I asked.

"Uh, good question. I am not too sure. Of course, she keeps a big scary-looking dog for protection I am sure, but I don't know if the Rott is friendly or not," she said.

"Well, sure. I can always use new clients. Go ahead and pass along my contact information," I said wondering what Cindy might be like in person.

About a week later, I got a call from an unknown number. I always answer those. The first rule of good business is always being available. People are impatient and fickle, so when they call, I answer it!

"Hello, this is Yvonne," I answered.

"Hi, this is Cindy Gill. Your friend Kristen referred me to you. I am in need of a pet sitter for my dog and cat." She said clearly and confidently, cutting to the chase.

"Yes, hi there! She mentioned you were looking. How nice to hear from you," I said, feeling a twinge of nervousness. A local celebrity requesting my services!

"I think I will need you in a couple of weeks, but I would like to meet you first," she said warmly.

"Oh sure, yes, I always do a meet-and-greet so that I can meet your pets and go over their routine. Then I'll have you fill out some light paperwork. Let me know when is good for you."

"I work most nights until 11 P.M., but I get a dinner break from 6:45-7:45 if you are free around then?" she asked.

"Yes, that'll work just fine. How about Thursday at seven?" I suggested.

"Perfect. I'll email you my address right now. Is this your email?" She read me the address Kristen gave her.

"Yep, that's it!" I said excitedly.

"Great. I am looking forward to meeting you!" she said.

"I am as well. I will see you on Thursday night at seven."

Thursday arrived before I knew it. I double checked my email to be sure I input her address correctly into my GPS and arrived at 7 P.M. exactly. I parked on the street in front of her house. It was a newer neighborhood with average sized homes. They all pretty much looked the same.

I felt nervous walking up to the door. I took a few deep breaths and knocked. In the pet sitting business, you don't ring doorbells because it usually startles pets much more than a knock, and they go bonkers. I certainly did not want her Rottweiler to go bonkers. I heard nothing, no barking or anything. She quietly opened the door and smiled broadly at me.

I thought she'd be taller. Maybe that's what they all say about TV people, and we just perceive them to be taller on TV. Standing in front of me, she was my height, about 5'4". It was weird to see someone I'd watched for years on TV now standing in front of me, and on her own doorstep no less.

"Hi Yvonne. Did you find it OK?" She smiled and held out her hand. I shook it.

'Yes, yes I did." I said, a bit star struck. She is only a newscaster, I reminded myself. It's not like she's Oprah or something.

"Great, come on in. I put Mona outside so she wouldn't go crazy when you arrived. She's normally great, but with new visitors she can get so excited!" Cindy shut the front door.

I followed her through the house to the back patio sliding doors. "There she is!" Cindy smiled and opened the sliding glass door where a Rottweiler was jumping around, squealing with excitement to see a visitor. Mona ran past Cindy and immediately began sniffing my shoes, my legs, and my crotch. I patted her on the head lightly. She looked intimidating, but I could tell she was a sweetie.

"Gosh, I am so sorry! She gets really excited whenever new people come over!" Cindy apologized for the excessive attention Mona was giving me.

"No problem," I said, stroking Mona's back. "Most dogs do the same thing. At least she doesn't jump up—she's pretty big!" I tried to make Cindy feel more at ease.

"Yes, she is a good watch dog, but I have her trained not to jump on guests!" Cindy said proudly. "Oh, and Donald is hiding right over there. He'll probably hide most of your stay; it takes him a while to warm up to strangers." Cindy pointed to a fluffy brown cat tail behind a curtain in the far corner of the living room.

"Can I get you a water or soda?" she asked, heading into the kitchen.

"Sure, I'll have a water. That'd be great, thanks." I said and took a seat on the couch. She handed me a glass with ice water in it. As I took a sip, Mona put her head on my thigh, staring up at me with big, dreamy brown dog eyes.

Cindy took a seat on the edge of a leather recliner facing me. She sipped her water and we began to talk about all the duties the pet sit would entail—feeding, exercise, sleeping arrangements, and the times she would depart and arrive. We discussed where the key would be hidden and the payment. We toured around her three-bedroom home. She showed me where I would be sleeping (in the guest bed). She kept the dog and cat food in the pantry. She showed me where the cleaning supplies were located in case there was a potty accident. We were lost in the details when she looked at her watch and realized she had to be back at work in fifteen minutes.

"I better get going, but please let me know if you have any questions, or if there is anything I missed," she said, putting our water glasses down in the sink. "I think I covered it all, what do you think?" she asked.

"Yes, we went over everything. I'll leave you this agreement. Fill it out, and leave it with your payment on the counter when you depart for your trip." I advised. "Don't forget to text me where you hide the key." I reminded her.

"Will do." She assured. "Yvonne, thank you so much! I am so glad Kristen referred you! I have a good feeling and Mona loves you already!" She seemed happy and relieved. She hugged me goodbye and I went on my way.

Driving away, I felt really confident about the upcoming pet sit at Cindy's place. Her pets were relaxed and she seemed super warm and friendly, just like on the news. Her house wasn't large or fancy inside or outside, just a typical middle class feel with normal neighbors. I was surprised she didn't have security cameras. Surely, being in the public eye as she was, that would be a safeguard.

Aside from having to greet myself in her huge floor to ceiling mirror every day, which was an understandable accessory for a newscaster, she wasn't much different than my average client. Mona and Donald were great pets and my stay there was rather uneventful. There was one thing though - a gift box on her dresser with an opened card. Curiosity got the best of me and I opened the card and discovered she would be moving soon, "Congratulations on your new endeavor! Good luck in Cali!" was scribbled inside. I knew before the public knew that she'd be moving out of state soon. As much as I'd wished there would be more juicy details to discover, there wasn't anything out of the ordinary around the house.

On my last afternoon there, a Sunday, I packed up, locked up her place and headed home. I jumped in bed once I arrived home, shut off my mobile phone and took a nap. Hours later I was startled awake by my doorbell ringing furiously. I rolled out of bed and ran downstairs to peek through the hole. It was my sister, Kellie. I swung open the door. She looked mad.

"Cindy got a hold of me and she said you still have her key and she is unable to get into her house because you locked the house-to-garage door. She only has her garage opener, not her key so she can't get in." *Oh shoot*, I thought. I forgot to re-hide the key. *Damn.* Kellie spun around and stormed down my driveway angrily. I later found out Cindy and her "team" called my sister a few times which she found annoying enough to get in her car and drive over to my place.

I closed my front door, then immediately called Cindy. "Hi Cindy, this is Yvonne. I am so sorry I locked you out of your place!" I said, embarrassed, still trying to wake up fully from my nap.

"No problem, but I have to be on air in two hours," She said, sounding to-the-point. "I need to get into my house soon!" Cindy laughed a little, making an effort not to sound angry, but I could tell she was annoyed.

"I'll be right over!" I said and hung up the phone. I threw on some shorts and a tee and raced across town to her place. When I arrived, she was sitting on a bench on her front porch, talking on her mobile phone. I got out of my car and ran up the driveway with her key.

"Here you go, I am so sorry!" I held out the key in my hand.

"Thank you!" She whispered, holding her phone away from her mouth. She took the key. She told whoever was on the phone to hold on. "Thanks for saving me from having to call a locksmith." She said quietly, her big eyes looking directly at me. "I'm too cheap for that! Ha!" She added warmly, muffling her phone with her hand.

"I hear ya!" I said. "I am glad I was able to just drive right over," I said, feeling silly.

"I have another trip upcoming; I will let you know the details. I'll shoot you an email this week." She said. "I've got to finish up this call and get going to work." She stood up from the bench.

"No problem! I am so sorry again! I'll look for your email." I waved and turned to head to my car parked on the street.

I pet sat for Cindy a couple of times after that. A couple months later I watched the farewell tribute to her long run as the nightly news anchor on TV. While the public was probably surprised by the news, I already knew that she'd be moving to California. I thought about how much taller she seemed on TV and how I almost made her late for the nightly news. I can officially say I pet sat for a local celebrity once and she was nice and normal, just like she seemed on TV.

7

THE TOILET WATER FLOOD

It is always nice to gain a new client directly from an existing one. One great way I was able to really expand my business was to do a good job and clients would mention me to their neighbors and friends. My website is a great tool but nothing beats word-of-mouth, especially in a personal service industry. People are always more comfortable hiring you when they've gotten a firsthand recommendation from others.

I was housesitting for a prominent client—Cindy, the local anchorwoman on the nightly news. I was outside the front of Cindy's home watering her flower-filled planters when the neighbor across the street walked up to me waving and smiling. She looked to be in her early-70s. She seemed so thrilled to be about to meet me as if, I too, was a celebrity who also pet sat for people on TV. She could see that my hands were full with the garden hose and she introduced herself excitedly.

"Hi, I'm Marsha, I live right over there across the street." She turned and pointed at her house, which looked almost exactly like the house I was staying at. I smiled, but before I could respond she went on, "I guess you are Cindy's pet sitter? Well, I also have been looking for someone to stay at my house and watch my pets." She smiled but seemed exhausted by her own excitement. "I have a mutt— well, a lab-mix—and a little Maltese as well as a tabby cat. They are all great pets, I tell you!" She adjusted her glasses behind her ear. "You must be really trustworthy if Cindy has hired you, I know she doesn't just hire anyone! Especially in her position, on the news and everything, ya know." She said cheerfully.

"Yes, a friend referred her, and she met me and checked my references and everything," I told her confidently. Marsha and I chatted a bit more, then I gave her my phone number and she walked back across the street to her house.

She called me later that night and before I knew it she booked me to stay at her house with her dogs, Scooby and Frank, and her cat, Lady. What an effortless way to gain a new client, I should have stood out front of Cindy's home and watered her plants for longer, I could have gotten the whole neighborhood as clients.

The first couple of stays at Marsha's house went well. Scooby and Frank were pretty relaxed.

Unfortunately, Scooby would always get diarrhea in the kitchen each time I'd stay there. It must have been a form of separation anxiety, that poor dog. I was getting tired chiseling up dried dog diarrhea off of the kitchen tile and I was thinking I might not want to stay there anymore if the situation didn't improve a bit. Marsha's tips of $5 were not quite sufficient enough for me to spend what seemed like hours cleaning up diarrhea. Back in those days, I was obscenely inexpensive and very overbooked, so tips were much appreciated, especially when going the extra mile in situations such as this. I'd say chiseling dried diarrhea off of the tile definitely merits a generous tip.

Tip-gripes aside, if I'd known what was going to happen on my final stay at Marsha's house the last thing I would have complained about would be a little bit of dog diarrhea.

It was a Friday night, and I was rushing to feed and poop the dogs and get out of there so I could get to a charity function I had planned to attend. I showered upstairs because I preferred the master shower to the little dinky guest shower downstairs. After my shower, I used the restroom at the top of the stairs and for some reason, the toilet was running. It wasn't clogged, just running. I tinkered with it a bit but it didn't stop. I figured eventually it would stop on its own and be fine as water didn't seem to be filling the base at all. I hurried down the stairs in a rush to finish getting ready for the event. I let Scooby and Frank outside one last time to do their business and I left to go to the event.

I arrived back to the house a few hours later. I eagerly slid off my high-heels and went upstairs to check on the cat and be sure there were no dog-potty accidents anywhere. I was always afraid Scooby would decide to spread his diarrhea bouts beyond just the kitchen tile. As I approached the bathroom at the top of the stairs, I could still feel the carpet beneath my feet, except instead, it felt like a soggy lawn after a good rain — soaking wet!

"*Oh my god*!" I muttered in a panic as I flicked on the bathroom light to find the tile floor completely underwater, and water pouring down the slots in the floor vent. The toilet had not stopped running like I assumed it would and it had obviously been overflowing for hours. I stood there stunned. *Must stop! Must dry!* I thought as I spun around and ran back downstairs to the garage to find paper towels or a mop or *something* to clean up the floor, to stop it from traveling to the carpet or continue pouring down the vent.

I flung open the door to the garage and heard the sound of pouring water before I could actually see what was going on. I frantically frisked the wall for the light switch and pressed it. I looked up and my mouth went dry. Water was streaming from the garage ceiling vents onto the garage floor. There was so much water it caused the paint on the wall to bubble up full with pockets of water the size of baseballs. Obviously, this horrific scene was caused by the toilet overflow-vent situation from upstairs. In my panic, I somehow quickly found a mop and some towel rags and ran back upstairs to stop the flow.

Upstairs I threw towels down and walked across them on the tile in my already soaked stockings. I opened up the toilet tank lid and I was finally able to tinker with the chain and flapper just enough to get it to stop running. Finally, the overflow came to a trickle, then to a stop, but it was barely a relief. Marsha would be back in a few days, and I imagined her coming up her stairs to find a wet swamp of carpet throughout. *I'll never pet sit in this town again*, I thought as I imagined being blacklisted from pet sitter lists and websites. There were so many scenarios going through my head.

I ran back downstairs and put a bucket down in the garage to catch the overflow that was still cascading like Niagara Falls (OK, maybe not, but it was *bad*). I then frantically mopped and dried the bathroom floor.

It was then that I had a few minutes to notice the extent of the damage. The water had fully saturated under the baseboards and soaked the carpeting into the next room. Not only that - it seeped down through the walls somehow and into the guest room on the first floor creating small bubbles in the wall paint and wet carpet all along the downstairs guest room baseboards. I wouldn't have believed it if I hadn't seen it, and I almost didn't notice it, but there was a damp paint smell when I was downstairs in the guest room where I was to sleep.

Upon further examination in the garage, there was so much water pooling in the paint pockets that they were bursting and the white paint was flaking off onto the garage floor. Not only would I be chiseling dog diarrhea off the kitchen tile inside, I'd also get to chisel paint off the concrete of the garage. Thank gosh she took her vehicle to the airport and it wasn't parked in the garage! That was the *only* silver lining of this whole ordeal.

There was the soggy soaking wet upstairs hall, the wet baseboards and carpet in the adjoining room, paint chips and paint splotches on the damp concrete floor of the garage, the damp walls, carpet and baseboards of the downstairs guestroom. It was potentially thousands of dollars' worth of home damage. I was in a state of panic, and I remained that way for two whole days.

No time to take it all in. I knew I had to act fast; she was going to be home in three days. The garage concrete was soaked. There were white paint chips splattered everywhere. The upstairs carpeting was soaking wet…. I did my best to dry out the carpet with towels and then I found some house fans and aimed them at the soaked areas. The next day I went home and got more fans to dry out the garage and damp downstairs areas. I even used a hair dryer to dry the corners and baseboards where the water had pooled. I was a nervous wreck.

I met my Dad for brunch the next morning and I was barely able to eat because I was so worried about cleaning up the mess! I thought I might get sued. Actually, I thought for sure I'd get sued. I even thought I might be on the news, that somehow it'd slip to the news anchor across the street and she'd report a big story on it. Every negative thought imaginable was going through my head. *Maybe I could eat myself to death right here at this table*, I thought, and then no one could do anything to me. I only managed to eat half of my meal while barely paying any attention to my Dad across the table. After brunch, I headed back to the house where heaters and fans were on full blast around the clock. I still shudder to think what Marsha's electric bill must have been after my stay.

My panic and diligence paid off. I was able to get everything dry, and most of the paint chips scraped up off the concrete. The house still had a slight damp smell in the guest bedroom and the garage, but other than that it was a huge improvement from the scene on Friday night.

Still nervous, I wrote Marsha a nice little welcome-home note and left it on the kitchen counter before I left on Monday and I waited for her call. I told her that the furries had a great time. Of course, I chose not to tell her about the toilet water incident but I swore to myself that if she asked me directly I would confess to all of it.

And she called—three months later she called to ask me to pet sit for her again. I was shocked.

There was no mention of any damage in her house, water, paint chips or otherwise.

"Lucy, Frank, and Scooby just love you. We all do, and we'd love for you to come back and stay!" Marsha said, praising me.

"Oh gosh, I would love to stay again," I said, "but those dates I am already booked for. I am so sorry." I lied.

I was relieved she asked me back but I had to turn her down. I was completely terrified to stay there again. I was convinced that some other potentially career-killing fluke accident would occur there again. And plus, I was tired of cleaning up Scooby's dried shit off the tile floor.

A few months after that after she decided to sell that house and downsize to another home across town. She called yet again to use my pet sitting services but I informed her I didn't handle that area and I referred her to another sitter in her new area of town.

Thank god it was done. She had sold her house and I expected that at some point in that process she would have come to learn of the damage that the water caused, but she never brought it up. Apparently, no one noticed, or perhaps it had happened again, or it wasn't the first time when it happened to me. Either way, bullet dodged.

To this day, when I flush in a client's home, I wait for the toilet to stop running before I leave the bathroom. Better to be safe than soggy. Or sued.

8
THEY'LL NEVER KNOW

I wish I could say that all of my pet sits had been perfect successes and that everything was kept in perfect order, but you already know that would be a huge lie. I consider myself to be a competent, tidy and responsible person. I am not typically clumsy or destructive to things, but for whatever reason, there have been incidents where things have gotten damaged. Sometimes bad things happen to good pet sitters.

During my first few years of pet sitting, I learned a hard lesson about why not to invite people over. There are always the jokes about throwing big parties while pet sitting in someone's place. You know a party is good when something gets broken. Somehow, I've had sense enough to never throw a party at a client's house. But the truth is, it just takes one person to ruin something, and that person could be me or that person could be someone else. This time that person was my brother.

I was staying in a super nice place in an upscale part of town—lots of huge backyards and extra space between houses. It was my first stay at a new client's place. They just had one dog, a Shih Tzu (their Brussels Griffon had died earlier in the year). It was a two-week stint while they traveled to London and Italy.

I was so happy to get away from my college roommate and to have a big, nice place all to myself. The neighborhood was pretty quiet and far removed from major intersections or traffic. This is just perfect, I thought as I got settled in. A few days later, I invited two of my brothers over to watch a movie from my client's large movie collection. We settled on a movie, and I made popcorn and ordered takeout.

A couple hours later, as the credits rolled, we cleaned up the living room area and took plates and empty glasses into the kitchen. I was loading the dishwasher when the loud shatter of porcelain on tile startled me. I froze and feared the worst. I ran out into the hallway. Scattered everywhere were white and blue colored shards, but it didn't look like the black dishes we had been using. Ralph, the Shih Tzu ran over to sniff the shards then quickly moved on deciding there was nothing too exciting there.

My younger brother Aaron stood there stiff, his back was inches from an empty plate holder mounted on the wall. I gasped, "Oh no, you knocked the plate off the wall?" I stared at him in disbelief, feeling suddenly angry. These clients had collector's plates mounted all over their hallway walls, some looked really old. "Damn it! Damn it! Damn it!" I yelled angrily. He blinked at me and opened his mouth but hesitated to speak.

"I am sorry! The dog ran in front of me and I lost my balance and my shoulder hit it." My brother said looking at me with wide eyes, his face turning pink.

I suddenly felt bad, anyone could have made the same mistake, but why him? Why now? Why me? I knew I shouldn't have invited anyone over; I secretly scolded myself in my head. He bent down and picked up some of the larger shards. I grabbed the broom and dustpan from the utility closet down the hall. Once we had all the pieces in the dustpan there seemed to be a few that had some markings on them, like a branding of sorts.

I carefully pieced the shards together on the counter top and the words "Delfts Royal Sphinx Maastricht" and "Made in Holland" were visible from the back of the plate. Since there was clearly no way we could glue the plate back together to where it would look new, I thought perhaps I could find a replica or an original on eBay. There were just under two weeks left of my stay, so perhaps I could get it just in time to put it back up on the wall and no one would notice a thing! I was trying to remain positive as I powered on my laptop in the office down the hall.

"I will pay for it." My brother said as he stared at my laptop's startup screen, our youngest brother plopped down in the chair next to the desk with a smirk on his face, happy to not be the culprit of this whole disaster.

"We can split it," I said trying to be nice. "It can't be that expensive, right? It is just a plate! Maybe there is a replica or something that'll suffice?" I talked out loud, frantically pulling up eBay and nervously waiting for the website to load.

I typed in "Delfts Royal Sphinx" into the eBay search box and forty results popped up, I felt some relief. Right off the bat, I could see various photos of blue and white dinnerware - plates, vases and other glassware priced at $15, $30, $109, etc. I scrolled quickly down the page looking for a plate with a windmill scene on it to match the plate that was now in pieces. I found one! It was priced at $59.99 with a little "Buy It Now" button next to the price. I clicked on the listing and carefully examined all of the photos. It looked exactly like the broken plate except the stamp on the back was slightly larger on the seller's plate than the plate I was replacing. Everything else looked the same.

Since it was the only plate with a windmill scene on it I had to buy it—there was no browsing for a better deal. I needed to get that plate back up on the wall within days. I figured it probably was a replica since the rear stamps were so different, but it would likely never be scrutinized while sitting in it's holder as if nothing had happened. I clicked on the "Buy It Now" button. The website prompted me to log in and in a matter of minutes, I had the plate paid for and scheduled for delivery the next week. Now if it would only arrive on time and in one piece, I could breathe again.

Over the next week, I thought about the plate incident every time I walked up and down the hall and noticed the empty plate rack on the wall. I vowed that I would never invite unannounced guests over to a client's house ever again! Family or not, it was clearly a dumb move. It cost me sixty dollars, and could cost me my client!

On Sunday of my last week there, I got an email from the eBay seller that the item had been returned to them for insufficient postage, he apologized and said he had been having problems with his shipping scale calibrations. *"What?!"* I whispered in a panic as I stared at the computer screen, my mouth hanging open.

I typed my response and hit reply: I really need that plate this week, I am on a deadline. I can't believe this is happening.

He replied: I know, I am so sorry, I am going to take it to the post office and ship it out tomorrow when the post office opens. It should get there by Thursday.

I replied: OK. Please do. I need it by the end of the week. It is dire. Thanks.

I closed my laptop and leaned back in my chair, feeling deeply uneasy about the whole situation. The clients would be back in town late on Friday night. If the plate got delayed again for some reason then I would have to confess what happened to the client. A broken plate on the first stay? Surely they'd not hire a klutz like me again. There was no way I would tell them my brothers were over, without their prior permission. Ugh. I didn't have a good feeling, but there was nothing else I could do.

Thursday came and went and no plate. I tracked the package online and the box had arrived in the city that day, but it was not on the truck for delivery yet. It must be sitting in a bin somewhere. I was so mad. I was a nervous wreck that the plate would not arrive in time, nervous that it'd be damaged or incorrect. My negative spiral of thoughts kept me awake for hours that night.

On Friday, I went to work at my office job, but incessantly checked the tracking number all day long online. By 9 A.M. the tracking number had an updated status of "out for delivery," which meant that it was on the delivery truck itself and on its way. I felt a small ounce of relief. I checked at noon, then 1 P.M., then 2 P.M., then 3 P.M., and it had still not been delivered. So close, yet so far away.

At four o'clock in the afternoon, I left the office and headed to the clients' home. I pulled up to the house and there was no package anywhere. Maybe the delivery driver didn't recognize my name at this address since it was my client's, I thought. Maybe it got lost or stolen from the truck somehow. I had exhausted myself imagining horrible scenarios.

I began to pack up my things so I would be ready to depart around 7 P.M. I fed and walked the dog and started tidying up. An hour passed and I was certain I'd never get that plate. I looked at the empty plate rack on the wall as if it would give me the answer about what to do next. It told me nothing. The only thing I could hear was my stomach churning with guilt and shame.

At half past six, I began loading up my car with my belongings. I loaded clothes on hangers, my suitcase, Caboodle toiletries case, a bag of shoes and my work bag. As always, I waited till after I wrote them their welcome-home note to load up my fridge and freezer items. I was dreading that I'd have to include a note about the missing plate.

Fifteen minutes later I was done with the note. Feeling deflated, I simply said I accidentally knocked it off the rack while using the broom. I told them that I had ordered a replacement and it was on it's way. I reread the note to make sure it sounded good and it was the best it could be. I lay it on the counter and retrieved my cold foods and pantry items, locked up, hid the key under the mat and left.

As I came to the intersection at the end of their block, the shipping truck roared past me. Could it be!? I thought to myself. I did a U-turn to follow it. Sure enough, it stopped in front of my client's house. I parked my car and ran up to the truck to sign for the package. I retrieved the key from under the mat, entered the house and tore the package open eagerly. Would it be the right one? Would it be broken?

I unwrapped the plate from layers of thick bubble wrap and studied it. To my relief, it looked exactly like the plate that had broken. It was perfect. I placed it on the rack and it looked as though it had never left. I felt like a queen. I had successfully covered my own ass and retained a client I'd have otherwise probably lost. I took a moment to feel proud of that. Then I re-wrote the note, leaving out the bit about the broken plate, and left it on the counter. I crumbled up the old note and the plate packaging and took it with me. (Not smart to leave any evidence!) I locked up the house once again and hid the key under the mat. I ran to my car, got in, and headed home feeling accomplished!

The next morning, per my standard procedure, I texted the client to be sure they made it home okay. They made it home without delay and they gushed about how clean their house looked and how happy their Ralph was. They booked me for another stay a few months later. I pet sat for them for years after that. To this day, nobody knows about the extra guests, the broken plate and the fake replica except for me, you, and the dog.

9
ILLEGALS LIVING IN THE BACKYARD

There are sometimes special requests from clients. Usually, it's nothing too crazy, but people can be very particular about certain things they want to be done, and the ways in which they want their home and pets cared for.

I've given clients' pets distilled water, special water additives, specially cooked meals. I've watered entire yards manually and had to diligently look after certain plants and feed special plants special foods. I've had to take dogs to the vet, take dogs to their special dog park, mail clients bills on a certain day— you name it, I've done it. The pet sitter role encompasses much more than scooping kitty litter or walking the dog around the block.

It was a sunny May afternoon, and I had just arrived at a new client's home for the initial meet-and-greet. This client was referred by a friend of mine, and I was excited to work with them because I learned that they go out of town a lot, had great pets, and lived in one of the best neighborhoods in town.

I parked my car and glanced up and down the wide street to get a feel for the vibe there. Seemed upper-middle class. Big houses, but not disgustingly so. Calm, no barking dogs or gawkers and not a lot of cars parked on the street. If you want to learn about a neighborhood, take a look at how many cars are parked on the street. This area was mostly single family homes, young and old families perhaps.

Sally opened the door with a warm smile before I could even knock, her indoor-outdoor Maine Coon cat darted through her legs and out the front door as I approached. They were eager to meet their new pet sitter. Her husband, Jason, greeted me just as warmly. They were an attractive couple in their mid-thirties, at a guess. They were very excited about their upcoming extended vacation to Greece. We chatted for a while as I bent down to acquaint myself with their friendly and hyper Weimaraner mixed-breed dog, while their skittish yellow Labrador-mix ran and hid under the bed in their master bedroom.

After discussing the pet care routine, we ended up in the kitchen where Sally showed me the pantry, where the dog food and treats were kept secure out of the dog's eager reach. The conversation was wrapping up and I was asking my usual questions "Any neighbor issues?", "Anything that spooks your pets?", "Any plants indoor or out that you want me to look after?" That last question prompted Sally and Jason to pause and smile at one another in an awkward hesitation. I smiled, too, out of pure confusion, but still making an effort to be polite.

"Yeah, there are some special plants outside that we'll want you to water and keep an eye on." Sally finally said flashing me a stiff grin.

"Let's go outside and we'll show you," Jason said as he unlatched the lock on the kitchen side door. The three of us walked outside. Their yard backed up to a large wide open space, it was nice and private except for the neighbors on each side. He led us to a large greenhouse in the far corner of the yard, hidden behind tall bamboo stems. This seemed strange to me until we walked into the greenhouse I looked at the plants. I noticed a majority of them looked exactly like marijuana leaves. Before I knew it, I blurted out, "Are these pot plants?" They both quickly shushed me and we all muted our nervous laughter.

"Yes, they are. This is our special plant experiment. We hope you don't mind watering them but if you feel uncomfortable, we understand." They both looked down and then back up directly at me. I was stunned. I tried not to make eye contact while I pondered the situation.

I'm not a prude by any means, but new clients asking me to stay in their home and care for their illegal growing operation was a bit much. I haven't been around pot very often in my life, so to know two seemingly normal people growing it in their backyard floored me.

I reminded myself that it was their backyard and not mine. I suppose if somehow the wrong person stumbled on it back there I could always feign a complete unawareness of it. Not my property, not my problem, right?

After a few minutes discussing the care of the plants, which was easy care at that, I agreed to do the job. I would care for their special plants and keep it all a secret. We chatted a bit more out on the back lawn and headed back into the house. I had them fill out my two-page agreement, with no mention of the greenhouse, just in case. Too bad I was so young and dumb, I failed to ask for extra payment for this special duty.

I left with their key, payment, and paperwork, ready to do the pet sit. I tried to ignore the fact that I would be engaging in illegal activity for a couple of weeks. I figured I'd hope for the best. What was the worst that could happen?

Several weeks later, I returned to begin my stay. Everything was going smoothly until day three. There was a knock on the door. Was it Jehovah's Witnesses? They always seemed to show up wherever I am pet sitting. Always during the 10 A.M. hour, and sure enough, it was half past ten. I rolled my eyes and opened the door. A petite older woman was standing there, smiling widely.

"Hi there, I—my name is Linda, and I am pretty sure my dog is trapped in your backyard!" she said excitedly.

"Oh really?" I said. "Come on in." I opened the door wider for her to enter. "I am pet sitting here. My name is Yvonne," I informed her.

"Hi Yvonne, so nice to meet you! I am so sorry! My little Yorkie, Buster, saw a squirrel and he squeezed under your side fence. He just loves squirrels!" She laughed.

"Oh, I know how that goes." I laughed with her and shut the door behind us. I lead her toward the side door near the kitchen. Then it struck me: I was leading her directly outside to where the pot plants were hidden. I couldn't do that and risk being found out. I had to think fast.

"Um, I think this lock is broken." I pretended to struggle with the bolt on the side door. I gave her a helpless look.

"Let me try it," she said and before I could protest, an audible click indicated that it had unlocked.

"Oh, gosh! Maybe I was turning it the wrong way, or you just have good luck!" I gushed while screaming inside, hoping her dog would be right at the door when she opened it.

He wasn't. "You know, I haven't poop scooped in a few days, let me go back there and get your pup. I don't want you to step in anything!" I demanded.

"Are you sure? It is no problem, I can get him." Linda looked at me with a blank stare.

"No problem! Allow me." I stepped outside.

"Just call him; I am sure he'll come right away," she assured.

"Buster! Buster!" I yelled once I walked around the side to the backyard. "Buuussster," I yelled again loudly and eagerly.

Luckily, Buster knew his name and was apparently exhausted from jumping up and down at the bottom of the tree after a squirrel. He slowly ran over to me panting heavily. I was relieved. I scooped him up in my arms as he licked my chin excitedly and I took him inside.

"Look who I found!?" I smiled and handed off Buster to Linda.

"Oh, you silly boy!" Linda let out a sigh of relief and hugged him in her arms. "Thank you so much!" she said. "What sort of special plants do they have in the back?" she asked, pointing to the bottom of my notes on the counter near us. It read: "special exotic plants in the back—don't forget!"

I froze.

"Oh! Yes, those. Um...Um...Hmm. I'm not sure what they are called exactly, but they require a special water schedule," I lied, hoping she wouldn't ask any more questions. I grabbed the paper and shuffled it under some other instruction sheets.

"That is interesting. Can I see them? I know about all different species of plants. I am an avid gardener!" she gushed, as Buster struggled to get free from her arms.

"I can take you back there another time. I really need to get the yard poop-scooped!" I said firmly, hoping she would take the hint.

"OK. I will stop by later in the week. I'll bring my camera that way if I can't identify them immediately I'll be able to find out if I snap a few photos!" She turned to walk up the hall toward the front door. "I am always looking for new species of plants that tolerate this climate!" She said excitedly.

"Oh OK. Great." I said as my stomach dropped. I followed her to the front door.

"Sorry about Buster getting into the yard! I am so glad you were home!" she said.

"No problem!" I said. "Have a great Sunday!" I waved goodbye and shut the door.

"Please don't let her return," I whispered to myself as I walked back to the kitchen in the rear of the house.

A couple of days passed and I hadn't forgotten about the incident when the doorbell rang. I jumped and my heart began to race.

I peered through the peephole and saw that it was Linda again. The dogs were going crazy barking, but I didn't open the door. I hid in the master bedroom, waiting for the barking to die down. It finally did. Whew, close call!

A few hours later it was time for the nightly dog walk, and I leashed up both dogs and headed outside. We walked for a couple of miles and were headed back when I saw Linda approaching us straight ahead. Oh God, how am I going to dodge her now? I thought, my heart raced. I got the feeling that Linda was one of those nosey neighbors, always meddling in other's private affairs.

"Hi, there! Yvonne—right? I stopped by earlier but no one answered. Perhaps you were out back watering those plants!" Linda exclaimed. "I have my camera with me and I'd love to see them!" she said cheerfully.

I only wished I could be as cheerful. "Oh, perfect," I said, trying to think up a way to dissuade her.

"You know, I am so glad we are almost back home now, because I have not been feeling well all day," I lied. "I am looking forward to toilet time when I return." I smiled sourly. It was all I could do to make her feel so uncomfortable that she didn't want to come over right then, or ever.

"Well if you just open the side gate, I can let myself in and out." Linda rubbed my shoulder sympathetically. This woman was relentless.

"It is locked and I don't feel like finding the key right now, honestly." It was the truth. I looked at my watch, anything to not have to make eye contact with her.

"Oh, well...OK," she said, sounding defeated. "I hope you feel better," she said as she turned to walk into her own driveway a few houses down the street.

"Thanks! I hope so too!" I said feeling happy and relieved, and not sick. Ha.

I knew that would not be the end of her. I knew she would pop up again somehow in the last few days I was staying there.

It happened the morning I was packing up to leave. I only had my fridge items left to load up into my car, and I went inside for my last walk through to make sure I didn't forget anything else.

The doorbell almost sent me airborne. It was Linda. She had probably been watching me load up my car with all of my stuff and decided this was the perfect time to pounce.

I opened the door. "Hi, Linda," I said cutting to the chase. "I am sure you want to go in back and see the special plants, but unfortunately they were stolen a couple of nights ago." I tried to look upset and furrowed my brow, looking down at the dogs who had gathered to see who was at the door.

"What?" she asked with wide eyes. "Yes, they took them all. I don't know what the client will think. I feel really bad," I said, picking off the dog hair stuck to my tee shirt to avoid eye contact.

"Oh, my! That is awful!" She said. "Normally there is no crime in this neighborhood! That is unheard of!" she said, flabbergasted.

"I thought it was odd, too," I said, shaking my head with fake disbelief.

I was hoping she would leave me alone now. Linda was becoming a real pest.

"Did you file a police report?" she asked.

"I informed the homeowners, but they told me not to worry about it but to keep a lookout for anyone suspicious," I lied; I couldn't believe how easily it flowed from my mouth! I was starting to believe myself!

"I will keep a lookout too," Linda said. "Tell the Smith's they can call me if they need anything at all," she said.

What we need is for you to stop bothering us, I thought to myself.

"OK, I definitely will, thank you Linda!" I said trying to sound appreciative, but I really just wanted her to go away. "Bye, now!" I said and shut the door abruptly. I didn't care at that point, I just wanted to get my food and get on my way.

I left a few minutes later and texted Sally and Jason, telling them to call me as soon as they landed so I could tell them about their neighbor, Linda, and the crazy story I had to make up about the marijuana plants. I didn't want to waste any time and knowing nosey Linda, she'd bombard them the minute they pulled up into their driveway.

Sally called me a couple hours later after they landed. I informed them of the big lie I told to divert Linda. She laughed and admitted they should have warned me about Linda. She is the neighborhood meddler who concerns herself with everything that is not her business. All the neighbors know to avoid her whenever possible. Unfortunately, I did not.

A day later Sally told me she was getting inundated with emails from neighbors about the plant theft. Neighbors wanted to know what happened and what sort of plants were "stolen." Sally discovered that Linda had shared the phony theft on the neighborhood's online listserv mere hours after I departed.

Sally minimized the scare by responding to neighbors that the plants were just sentimental Bearded Irises from her deceased mother that she wished to keep thriving. They were in some colorful pots so it was probably just some bored teenage pranksters in the area, she speculated in her response on the listserv. Sally mentioned it was nearing the end of the school year and that is usually when these pranks happen. And with that, she successfully diffused the whole situation. The last thing she wanted was curious neighbors poking around her yard, or for the police to get alerted.

10
CELEBRITY GUEST

It just so happened that one of my favorite New Mexico clients worked in the film industry. Movies in New Mexico, you ask? Yes, movies in New Mexico. The state provides tax cuts and discounts galore to movie and TV projects filmed in the state. You'd be surprised how many TV shows and films are shot in New Mexico each year because of these incentives. So yes, my clients were prominent in the film community, living in a mansion on a sprawling ranch in the valley of Albuquerque, New Mexico.

I had pet sat for them a dozen times or so when I arrived to start my next stay. I arrived on a gorgeous Saturday in August. I punched in the secret gate code and pulled in. Their King Charles Spaniel, Boba, and Poodle, Pete, running up to my car as I drove around back. I retrieved their garage door opener and keys from the usual hiding spot inside a planter pot in the back of the house. I opened one of four garage doors and pulled my car inside. Boba and Pete jumped up on me to greet me as I opened up my trunk and began unloading my luggage and grocery bags.

After about ten minutes of unloading, I closed the outer garage doors and headed to the kitchen to load my perishables into the fridge. I glanced at my welcome-home note in the usual spot on the end of the marble island in the kitchen. I read it, nothing unusual except for the part that said there was a guest staying in the guesthouse across from the pool. The pool was in front of the kitchen windows, directly across it was the guest house. I glanced over at the guesthouse and noticed some lights on inside. Something struck me about the note; it specifically said: "please do not disturb the guest."

Typically, these clients are very forthcoming about any and every change that could possibly interfere with my stay. For some reason, this time they waited until I arrived to leave me with this note and a "do not disturb" order on it as well. It seemed unusual especially since the other time they had guests in the house while I was there was announced well beforehand and not a secret. Granted they were relatives passing through for a night but still, at least I was given a heads up that time. This time seemed odd.

Later that night, I sprawled out on their couch after dinner to catch Pulp Fiction on one of their bazillion cable TV stations. Mia Wallace and Vincent

Vega looked bigger than life up there dancing on the big fancy flat screen, in all of their superstar glory. I wondered what it would be like to be in front of a camera, to be a celebrity, a superstar. Then it dawned on me: unannounced guest, not to be disturbed staying in the guest house of movie producers?

"There must be a celebrity staying in that guest house!" I said out loud and jerked upright on the couch. Boba and Pete looked at me excitedly quickly stirring from their slumber on the couch next to me.

I pressed pause on the TV remote and sat there for a minute pondering my curious thought. I got up and walked out to the kitchen, peeking around the corner to see the guest house through the kitchen windows without getting noticed. It was dark outside and I could see lights on in the guesthouse. I quickly turned off the kitchen lights so I wouldn't be spotted stalking whatever celebrity was staying over there, just across the pool. I wondered who it could be. I looked hard. I squinted to see if I could tell who it was through the partially open blinds. Was it one person or two? I could see nothing from across the pool.

Maybe it was someone filming a movie here who needed a place to sleep for a weekend? Maybe a weekend getaway? Maybe it was a celebrity visiting another celebrity? Who was filming in town recently?

I looked up the film projects in town on the NMFILM website, there were various projects in progress that summer and the likes of Scarlett Johansson, Samuel L Jackson, Morgan Freeman,

Johnny Depp were a few of the names I stumbled across. Maybe it was someone related to the Breaking Bad cast that needed a place to stay for a weekend? You never know. Brian Cranston could be forty yards away from me right this minute. Or Johnny Depp! Maybe it's Julia Roberts—perhaps she needed a break from her ranch in Taos and she wanted to come into the state's biggest city for a few days?

With all of the possibilities dancing in my head, I decided I would have to go outside and investigate. I slipped on my flip flops and went out the side door so that I couldn't be directly seen if I went out near the pool. I walked around the side of the house. I could see shadows inside the guesthouse bedroom. There seemed to be only one person in there, but I wasn't sure. I held my breath as I walked up to the side of the window and peeked in. I could see the back of someone's head. They were reading a book but I couldn't tell which book—oh wait, no—it was a script.

"Oh. My. God," I whispered to myself. Someone reading a script! The someone was obviously a man, because his shoulders were broad and his hair was an unkempt mess of curls and matting. *Curls and matting, hmm, what celebrity would have hair like this?* And in an instant, it came to me. I gasped, spun around, and carefully jogged back around the side of the house so as not to get caught. Meanwhile, Boba and Pete were now alongside me, barking because I was acting strangely. I shushed them while trying not to stumble over my own feet in the dark. I finally made it to the side door and leaped inside, the dogs followed. I shut the door and locked it and let out a sigh of relief to have returned from my snooping undiscovered.

I ran to the couch to get my phone, and called up my friend Brigitte, I had to tell someone this news!

"Guess what?" I blurted out after she finally answered.

"What?!" She sounded partially horrified. I guess I would be, too, if my best friend called me with a frenzied tone.

"Johnny Depp is about forty yards from me, right this second. He is staying here in the guest house where I am pet sitting!" I gushed.

"You're shitting me!" Brigitte shrieked. "I am coming over right now!" she said excitedly.

"No!" I shrieked. "I could lose these clients if we bug him!"

"What? How?" Brigitte was perplexed.

"They specifically put in their instructions not to disturb the guest in the guesthouse. They've never been so specific before so I know they are serious," I said. "And I'd like to spend more summers in their massive house, in their massive pool, with their wonderful pets. It's an easy gig, and I'd like to keep it!" I shouted. Why was I shouting?

"Okay, okay, but you can't just call me up with this news and expect me to be cool. I mean you only live once! We should go over there and seduce him! Who cares if you lose one good client, you have lots more!" Brigitte said.

She was right. I had more clients than I could handle but there was no way the perfectionist in me was going to purposely fuck up this good gig. "Okay, how about you come over and knock on his door and pretend that you thought it was the main house." I could hardly believe the words coming out of my mouth. "Then *you* can seduce him and tell me all about it." I figured that'd shut her up.

"I will do it. Give me the address," Brigitte said confidently. She did have a way with men, but I couldn't believe she was going for it.

"You can't be serious. What if he's an asshole celebrity and slams the door in your face or something?" I asked. I was trying to get her to think about the possible negatives of the situation. I really didn't want to let her talk her way into coming over. As exciting as it could be, it could also be a letdown.

"Well then, nothing lost, nothing gained and we'll know he's an asshole celebrity then," Brigitte said. "I'm putting on my shoes now, tell me the address," she demanded.

I hesitated for a minute, then I decided to give her the address and gate code. I told her to park in front, by the guest house. "But I am not involved in this; you have to pretend that you knocked on the wrong door," I stipulated.

"I know. I know. I promise I'll knock on the guesthouse door looking for you. I'll have a whole scheme planned in my head by the time I arrive. Trust me, if there is any question from your clients, it won't be because of you. All my fault!" She sounded devious and convincing.

I was unsure of the whole plan, but I trusted her. Brigitte was a bit impulsive, but she was trustworthy. I knew she'd follow through with her plan and try her very best not to get me into trouble. She was a loyal friend.

Thirty minutes later she arrived. I could see the reflection of her headlights cast through the front windows of the house. She pulled through the gate and parked in front of the guest house. I stood in the dark foyer of the main house, peering out the front windows while the dogs watched me, wondering what the hell was going on.

She got out of her car and walked up to the guesthouse door, at which point she was out of view. All I could do was put my ear to the glass trying to hear anything. I heard nothing. I knew if I opened the door the dogs would bark and dart out and at this point in the night, I was not going to risk it. I sat there, wondering what was going on. Minutes passed.

Ding Dong the loud doorbell sounded. I startled alert and stood up. The dogs began barking emphatically. I had been lost in thought, sitting on a chair by the front door.

I looked out the window. It was Brigitte at the door. I opened the door while Boba and Pete barked and weaved around my legs excitedly.

"Hi." I looked at Brigitte as I swung open the door. She put her finger in a shushing motion over her mouth. I closed the door behind her. Then she talked.

"That is *not* Johnny Depp!" she said in an annoyed tone. "And I need a drink!"

"What? Really?" I asked, puzzled.

"No, his hair is similar and everything else, but that guy is about twenty years younger and, well, less famous," she said, plopping down on the piano bench a few feet away. "But my God was I nervous as I walked up to the door and knocked. I suddenly forgot everything I had planned to say!" She laughed and sighed loudly.

"I'm so surprised!" I said as I thought of what I had seen earlier. "I thought for sure that was him. Maybe I wanted it to be him." I felt a little bad for luring her across town with false hopes.

"Well, he does look similar. But he is no Johnny Depp!" Brigitte patted Pete's fluffy head as he eagerly awaited her attention.

"What did you say to him?" I asked walking toward the kitchen. "What can I get you to drink?" I asked.

"Sparkling water with a big splash of vodka if you have it?" She followed me into the kitchen. I grabbed a jumbo sized bottle of Ketel One vodka from the bar next to the kitchen. "I just asked if I had the right house and then I didn't know what else to say when he pointed me to the main house so I just told him he looked really familiar." She leaned forward on the kitchen island and rolled her eyes. "I mean, how dumb was that? I used the oldest pickup line in the book! I could've said anything at all and I came up with that? What has happened to me?" She whined with disappointment.

"Well is he at least cute? Maybe we could go over there later after a few of these." I handed her the requested cocktail. "Cheers!" I raised my glass to hers. She took a long sip.

"Where were we?" She set her glass down.

"Was he cute, at least?" I sat down on the bar stool.

"Actually, he was pretty cute, now that I'm over the fact that he wasn't who I was expecting." She smiled as a mischievous thought entered her mind.

Two hours, and several vodka sodas later, we were skinny dipping in the pool. We were being obnoxious and our laughter was echoing throughout the courtyard. It was almost ten o'clock when the double doors to the guest house flung open and Mr. not-Johnny-Depp walked out. We froze and stared at him. Luckily, our nudeness was underwater.

"I can hear you two over my radio," he said. We couldn't tell if he was upset or not.

"Sorry, we've kind of gotten carried away," I said, feeling embarrassed.

"It is no problem. It dawned on me that maybe it is a sign I should join you. I've been working all day. Would you mind?" He asked, looking up at the dark sky. "It is a beautiful night. That moon—"

"It is so bright, isn't it? I love the clear New Mexico skies," Brigitte said, "Sure, you can join us." She looked at me, then she looked away before I could give her a protesting look. I wasn't going to protest; the guy was hot.

"I'm Yvonne. What is your name?" I waved at him from the middle of the pool. "I think you met Brigitte earlier." I looked at Brigitte, she was floating on her back at the far end of the pool, her nipples surfacing the water.

He pulled off his tee shirt. "My name is Cole." He looked at me and smiled. He slid off his shoes by pressing on each heel with the opposing foot. "I'm staying here for a few weeks," He continued.

"Nice to meet you," I said. "I am just here for the week, pet sitting. How do you know Olivia and Alex?" I asked.

He walked around the side of the pool and got in where the submerged stairs were. "I know them through colleagues in the film industry," he said. "This pool is so warm!" He sank down into the pool up to his neck.

"Yeah, it's the perfect temperature, isn't it?" I swam to the stairs passing Cole in the water. "I'm going to go get some refills, who wants something?" I asked, stalling in the water to wait for their responses before getting out.

"What are you two drinking?" Cole asked.

"Vodka-sodas, of course." Brigitte swam over to Cole.

"Sure, that sounds great. Count me in," he said, smiling at Brigitte.

I got out and grabbed our empty glasses sitting next to the pool and headed inside to mix the next round of drinks. As I poured and mixed I could hear laughter coming from the pool. Sounded like Cole and Brigitte were hitting it off. Maybe the trip across town would provide more than a swim in the pool and some vodka-sodas for Brigitte.

I returned to the pool with my towel wrapped around me. Brigitte and Cole were talking about sports teams, in which I had no interest. I handed them their drinks as they still were in deep sports talk. It was one of the last things I remembered.

The next morning, I awoke feeling like I'd been lying in the Sahara Desert without water for days, maybe weeks. My body ached with dehydration, my eyes felt like they had pebbles rolling around in them, and my mouth was parched. There was a full glass of water next to my bed which I must have poured because it was in the same glass I like to use, their Purdue University glass.

Of course, I had a headache as well, but thankfully it wasn't too bad. I rolled myself out from the blankets, sat up and slipped into my flip flops, which were sitting on the floor beside the bed. I was dressed in my pajamas, which I vaguely remember putting on the night before. I strolled out into the kitchen and looked at the huge clock on the wall, it was a few minutes past eight.

Boba and Pete heard my flip flops slapping the hardwood floor and I could hear them excitedly stirring in the laundry room where they slept at night. I opened the door and let them out. I wondered where Brigitte ended up, because I noticed her purse still on the counter in the kitchen. I let the dogs out the back door so they could do their business in the yard. I then went to the poolside glass patio door to look out before opening it. There sleeping on the patio couch was Brigitte and Cole, snuggled together under a towel. Somehow the bottle of vodka had made its way outside too. It sat on the patio table, less than half full.

I opened the door and walked out.

"Hey, you two. I guess we drank a lot last night?" I said, as they groaned and turned over on the couch. I wondered if they were feeling as bad as I was. "That bottle was almost full!" I said, trying to sound cheerful and ignore the pounding behind my right eye.

"Ugggghhhh. Yeah, we drank too much!" Brigitte rubbed her brow and squinted in my direction. She looked over at the bottle on the table. "Good God!" She sighed, seeing how empty the bottle was. Cole put the towel over his face and let out a deep breath. It was clear all three of us got our butts kicked by Mr. Ketel One, and bad.

An hour later Cole headed back to the guest house and Brigitte and I chatted in the kitchen a bit before she left for a hair appointment. Later that day I looked up Cole on the Internet Movie Database (IMDb) online and sure enough, he was a working actor, a B-list celebrity who had been in some major movies acting in smaller roles.

Brigitte and Cole hung out a few times over the next few weeks until he returned to Los Angeles, where he lived. To this day when I see him in movie roles, I always think of that fun night in the Valley mansion pool.

11
HIDE YOUR VALUABLES—
I MEAN, HIDE YOUR FOOD

While pet sitting requires a lot of focus on the animals, there are other aspects to it too. One of the small perks of staying in other people's homes is there is usually an offering of food. Most clients specifically say, "Please help yourself to anything in the pantry or fridge." If I was a starving college student they might think again before saying that, because they might come home to an empty fridge and pantry, but I'm not. Maybe that's why they call again, and again: they're happy not to see a barren pantry when they come home from vacation.

I will typically bring my own food to my house stays, because there are particular things I like in my diet. That said, it's always nice to see what other people eat, and I'm fascinated by the things people have in their fridges and pantries. I am amazed by how ancient some items are. An expiration date of 2014? Seriously, purge some of your food items on occasion!

One time I became physically ill after nibbling on some bad lunchmeat from a client's fridge. I was working as an Executive Assistant for the CEO of a corporation in Albuquerque, New Mexico. I spent the next day home sick from work when it dawned on me between bathroom visits to check the package because it might be the culprit. It was many weeks past the use-by date. It's no wonder that I don't eat meat anymore.

Another curious fact is that nine times out of ten, people have spices in their pantry that are years past their use by date. Sometimes decades. Yes, it's true. Check your condiments and spices right now and I guarantee that at least forty percent of them are expired. Luckily, old spices don't seem to do a number on the digestive system like animal products do.

I've also discovered some great groceries by sampling the offerings in client's kitchens. As a foodie, it has been awesome to see what other people buy. Interesting hummus flavors, tasty protein shakes, sweets, flavored tortilla chips, smoky cheeses, fun cereals, delicious meal bars, tasty teas and rich coffees. And the list goes on. Not that I devour these things, but I will usually have little samplings—just enough to decide if I want to put it on my own grocery list.

My one weakness is sugar. I hate it (but secretly I love it) when people leave out cookies, candy, or other sweets. They taunt me my entire stay. I once had to hide a bowl of chocolates for fear I'd eat them all. I hid them so well, I forgot about them. It was almost a week after my stay when the client called me up to ask what happened to their bowl of candy. I had to think for a minute before I remembered that I'd hid them under some towels in their linen closet.

A client left a sign on a big holiday tin of Mrs. Fields cookies on the counter. The note read: "eat me." *Are you sure about that?* I decided in my head that the client wanted me to eat every last one so they didn't have to. So, I did. At least they know what to expect the next time they put an "eat me" sign on something. When there's sugar involved, I'm all in. Don't say I didn't warn you.

One December I settled in for my week-long stay at a client's home. On day two I was excited to discover a box of cookies in their pantry. These were no regular cookies; these were chocolate-covered Joe-Joe's from Trader Joe's. If you've never had them, you should. Think chocolate-covered Oreos but with more character and decadence. I think I started drooling at the pictures on the box before I even opened it. According to the box, there were multiple flavors inside—chocolate, white chocolate, peppermint, peanut butter. I opened up the box and luckily one of the sleeves was already open. I feel like it's less noticeable if I sample from an already open item. At least, that's what I tell myself.

I bit into the cookie. It tasted like a Girl Scout Thin Mint on steroids. The chocolate coating and crunch filled my mouth. I let out an "mmmm" of pleasure as I continued chewing and took a couple more bites until it was gone. This was amazing; my taste buds were having multiple orgasms. I went back to the pantry for more, reopened the box, and had another, then another, then another. Before I knew it, the entire open sleeve had been consumed. I came to and put the box out of sight in the back of the pantry, ashamed of myself.

A day passed and I tried not to think about the cookies. The problem with sugar is that it's addictive—once you cave in and indulge, your body wants to keep the party going, even when it's past 2 A.M. And we all know nothing good happens after 2 A.M. My body wanted more and before I knew it, it was two days later, and I was sitting on the couch, devouring what was left of those amazing cookies.

Sometimes I'll get carried away with a food item that I discover in a client's home. I will finish whatever it is, but I always replace it. Hey, I know how it feels to want something and go look for it, only to find it missing. Nobody likes that feeling.

Luckily, this client lived right around the corner from Trader Joe's. I figured I could easily just replace the cookies I ate with a new box. I'd eat one or two out of the new box so that it would match the original box—an easy fix.

I went to Trader Joe's the next night. The parking lot was crowded, but I managed to get a spot near the building. I picked up some things I needed and then began the search for the Joe-Joe's. They weren't in the sweets section. Certainly, I must have missed them. I made another trip down the aisle. There was still no sign of the orange and pink box. *Surely they're here somewhere*, I thought to myself, rounding the endcap for the third time. I decided to head to the seasonal holiday section, in case they were there. A quick glance of the shelves and there seemed to be every cookie on earth but not the special Joe-Joe's I was looking for. *This can't be so. It's the middle of December. They must have more of these cookies somewhere*, I thought, beginning to panic.

After circling the store several more times, I finally gave up and decided to ask an associate. "Excuse me," I said desperately when I spotted a guy in a Trader Joe's tee shirt. He twirled around with a warm grin across his face. His nametag said "Danny." I must have seemed panicked, I realized, but I got right down to business. "I am looking for the chocolate covered Joe-Joe's, do you have them? I can't find them anywhere," I asked hopefully.

"Oh, yes, someone asked about those earlier. I couldn't find them, either. You know, let me just double check in the back for you. There may be a straggler to two, but I am pretty sure we're completely out." I think I must have had a horrified look on my face because he ran off to the back before I could even respond (or cry).

I hung around the endcap by the registers, waiting for him to return, and decided a plan B was in order. Maybe I would try another location, even have him call over and reserve a box for me. Surely they wouldn't be out, too! This was the middle of December for God's sake. They couldn't possibly run out of seasonal items now! *Dammit, why did I eat that whole box?* I deserved this, and maybe next time I would have more self-control.

After a few minutes, which seemed like an eternity, Danny finally returned. "Hey there, you're in luck." I heard, and I spun around to find him holding one pink and orange box. "It was the last one," he said, handing me the box and smiling proudly. Relief filled me as I hugged and thanked him. I left the store and put the box safely in my client's pantry. I ate two to match the original box and left it alone for the last few days of my stay, despite being tempted.

Another lesson learned: never eat all of something unless you already have the replacement. And take special caution with seasonal items.

12
I'M A HOUSE SITTER, NOT A HOMEWRECKER!

It would be my fourth stay at their house. I was looking forward to watching their Labradoodle the most. Her name was Pippa, and she was full of energy. I always enjoyed my stays with her because I'd have to walk her around the neighborhood and she always got me going at a good pace. Yes, some dogs, they walk you instead of the other way around.

They requested dates immediately following a major surgery I had scheduled. I would not be able to walk Pippa, but I would be able to do any other duties they wanted me to do. They still agreed to book the stay because Pippa loved me, and they did too. I'd later find out just how much.

It was 5:50 P.M. when I pulled up on the street to park. I lollygagged in my car for a minute. I never want to be super early—it seems like an invasion of someone's time and space. I walked up to the door and rang the doorbell.

John and his wife Glenda were in their late fifties. They lived in an upper-class neighborhood with sprawling yards and wide streets. They were an average empty-nester couple with two kids in college. They were active in the community and had important careers. Their dog had become their main "child" now. John had me arrive a few weeks early to get the key and to show me the new routine with Pippa. She was not allowed into a special corner of the house that had become a problem potty spot. She was just out of the puppy stage and acting out on occasion by randomly peeing in a favorite spot inside the house. They had gated off the area around the bar in the corner of their living room so she could not soil there.

"Hi, there," John said as he opened the door. Pippa pushed beside him and jumped up to my waist and down again with excitement.

It was strange because you'd think she'd *not* be excited to see me. Because when she sees me, her parents are usually gone away for a week or more. But she was. She jumped on me ecstatically, a welcome that never gets old!

I'm pretty sure some pets are excited to see me because I give them more attention and affection than their actual owners do. I think this was the case with Pippa. She loved when I was with her because she was a people-dog, which means she prefers people to other dogs, so she badly desired time with people. I smothered her with time and affection.

Yes folks, sometimes you can hire a pet sitter to do more than just pet sit. Sometimes, a pet sitter can provide more time and attention than you do. Yes, I said it.

Anyway, back to the story.

I sat down on the loveseat near the entryway. Pippa was finally calming down on the carpet beside me. John asked if I would like a glass of water, sprite, or tea. I asked for tea. He poured me a glass of iced tea and sat next to me on the couch. We chatted for a while about the weather, Pippa, and their upcoming travels to the west coast. I reminded him that I couldn't walk Pippa for the five days I'd be there because their trip would be after my upcoming surgery. I was not supposed to exercise or have pressure on my arms, like leash tugs on a dog walk. Pippa loved to tug and pull me when on walks.

"If you don't mind my asking, what type of surgery are you having?" he asked with a curious and concerned look on his face.

"I'm having breast augmentation." I replied confidently. I was secure in my decision to get my breasts to look proportional to the rest of my body. If there were a workout to increase bust size I would have mastered it, but since there was not, surgery was the next best solution.

"Wow, really?" he asked, seeming genuinely puzzled.

I felt the need to explain. "I have worked hard on my body, and I'm happy with it, but there was one thing I couldn't change through diet and exercise, and it was my breast size," I said matter-of-factly. "I wanted my breasts to be in proportion with the rest of my body," I said, trying to sound nonchalantly confident, but fearing I was being judged. I suddenly felt a bit uncomfortable.

"I understand that." He nodded his head up and down. "If you need anything at all, don't hesitate to contact us," he said in an assuring tone, glancing down at my chest.

I would later discover he was completely turned on by the entire scenario.

The following week I completed my stay at their house with Pippa. It was a successful pet sit with no issues. A week after they returned from their trip, he called me.

"Hi Yvonne, this is John."

"Oh, hi," I said, wondering why he was calling me. Thoughts flew through my head: Did they not find the key to the house that I carefully re-hid? Was something wrong with Pippa? Did they have another vacation planned already?

"I just wanted to call to check on you and to see how you are doing after your surgery?" He quickly inquired. He sounded a bit nervous, but I didn't know him well and I wasn't sure.

"Oh, yes, I am doing OK. I'm still not allowed to lift anything heavy, but I am managing just fine." I replied, relieved that he wasn't calling due to some problem with the house or with Pippa.

"Well, that is great. I am so glad to hear." He sounded genuinely happy.

"Thanks," I said. "Luckily, I think the worst part is over."

"I would like to take you out to celebrate." He said, "I know it might sound unusual, but Glenda will be out of town on business for a week, and it wouldn't hurt to have some company. It would be our thank you for all the great care you've provided for Pippa, and a celebration that you had a successful surgery!" He sounded excited. I didn't want to rain on his parade, and after all, it was only dinner. No funny business. He was just a nice guy.

"Sure. That would be nice. What night were you thinking?" I asked, trying to remember if I had any solid plans later that week.

"Friday or Saturday night would work best, around seven if that works for you?"

"Ummm, how about Saturday night? I think that will be better than Friday, because I have a lot going on Friday afternoon." I proposed.

"That will work great," He said.

"Where did you have in mind? I'll meet you there," I said.

"Jinja restaurant, in the Northeast Heights." He said it definitively, as if he had already researched the options.

"That will be great. I love that place!" I said, feeling excited and spontaneously hungry.

"Perfect. I will see you there on Saturday at seven. I'll make the reservation under my name," He said

"Great. I will see you then. Goodbye." I ended the call and stared at my phone for a good minute. Was this OK? What if I drank too much or was too candid, would this client ever hire me again? What if there was total awkwardness and nothing to talk about? I mean, he was, like, my Dad's age.

I decided it would be the best thing to just do it. It would be a nice dinner and probably good conversation, and could potentially drum up future business or referrals. If it went terrible, worst-case scenario I'd lose a client and get a great meal. There are worse things in the world.

Saturday rolled around and I had actually been looking forward to the evening all week. Not because it was a romantic date—it wasn't in the least—I'm just a foodie, and I was looking forward to the delicious food and tasty cocktails more than anything. I just hoped the conversation flowed enough to not make the entire night awkward. There is something about bad or no conversation that makes an otherwise amazing meal taste mediocre. *Please let that not happen tonight*, I thought as I parked my car near the front door.

I arrived a few minutes late. He was standing near the host podium, looking down at his phone. He looked up as I entered and walked toward him.

"Hi!" He grinned ear to ear and put his phone into his back pocket.

"Sir, we are ready to seat you now." The host eagerly acknowledged my arrival and stacked up two menus in her hand, ready to show us to our table. John nodded and we turned to follow her to be seated. She sat us at a cozy booth in a corner of the restaurant. We slid around on either side of the table, not quite directly across from each other.

We began looking at the menus while our server brought us waters. It wasn't long until she approached to take our drink order.

"Hello, I am Tammy, and I'll be your server tonight, can I get you something to drink besides water?" She smiled.

Yes, please! "I'll have the Jinja Mule," I said, looking at John for approval.

"I'll have the same." He smiled at the server and rested his drink menu on the table. She wrote the order on her pad, smiled and swiftly walked away.

"I'm a sucker for a Moscow Mule." John took a sip of his water and looked at me.

"I like them too. They aren't too sweet, yet aren't too tart or strong," I said, sipping my water. "Let's hope their version is good."

We browsed the food menu and soon our Jinja Mules arrived. We placed our food orders and settled into a light conversation about how our weeks were going and the latest news and weather topics. Before long, we were two drinks in. The night was going well. Conversation flowed smoothly. I was trying not to be too revealing; I feel like no one ever wants to know too much about their pet sitter. He was being very flirty, I noticed. It was completely unexpected and I didn't know what to think about it. Was it just me? Was he simply a flirty person when he drinks? It didn't take me long to figure it out.

"So why, again, did you get your breasts done?" he blurted out between bites of glazed chicken. I could tell he was a bit intoxicated. I didn't know what to say. Was this the point where the night would take a turn for the worse? I hoped not. I took a long gulp of my drink.

"I worked out hard and I was happy with my body, but the only thing that was disproportionate to my body and butt were my breasts. I was flat-chested and there wasn't much I could do to increase my breast size, so I decided to have the surgery done," I replied, trying to sound as articulate as possible. "I am happy with how my body seems to be better proportioned now," I said and took a sip of my third Jinja Mule.

"I think that is wonderful," he said. "I know that probably wasn't an easy decision for you," He added.

"It was not something I'd ever imagined for myself," I said. "But I decided to take a risk and see how it would turn out. I am happy with the result so far," I said, looking down at my chest playfully trying to keep the conversation light.

We chatted a bit more and finished the last of our drinks. I looked at my watch, it was almost nine.

"Are you OK to drive?" he asked, noticing me glancing at my watch.

"Not quite yet, let's hang out here for a bit so I can sober up," I said, suddenly feeling embarrassed.

"Sure, no problem," he said. "I am enjoying your company."

"Yeah, this has been so nice. Thanks for dinner and the drinks. It was all so good!" I smiled, full and sleepy and tipsy.

"There is a great little Asian joint I go to in D.C. whenever I am out there for business. It beats this, you'd love it." He paused. "You know, I'll be out there in a few weeks, you should join me. You could stay in my hotel room. I would buy your ticket. There would be no expense to you." His eyes shifted around the room as he lowered his voice.

I was glad I was a bit tipsy, for the night had officially gotten strange. Even stranger was the fact that while he was offering all of this to me he thought that I might go for it, as if it were no big deal. I wondered if he had done this kind of thing before, perhaps many times before. Definitely many times before. I was stunned, but didn't want to make him feel bad, and I still needed to stay there for another half hour or so to sober up a bit before driving.

I took a sip of my water to stall and try to compose my response.

"Really?" I asked him. That was all I could come up with as the feeling of shock stirred the alcohol and food coma saturating my body.

He took a moment to respond. "Yes, really." He looked me directly in the eyes. I looked away.

I think he thought I was actually considering it. What I was considering was the assumption that I'd even go for it, the fact that he'd actually ask! It didn't seem like him to ask something like this. He seemed to be in a well-established, comfortable marriage with two grown kids. Why would he want to risk all of that? He couldn't be that unhappy, could he?

"Thanks for the offer but I—" I cut myself off mid-sentence and asked what I truly wanted to know. "Aren't you happy?" I was getting angry, but I tried not to let it show. This guy had a great life and seemed like a good guy, but he was not. So, this was why he wanted to take me out—to get into my pants. I hate being deceived.

He leaned back and adjusted his collar. "I am not that happy. Glenda and I have been together for over two decades. Marriage is hard. Often times we're disconnected," he said, letting out several sighs. I could tell he was telling the truth. Suddenly he seemed rather flustered. He looked down, his cheeks blushing.

"I think you are handsome and a good person, but you are also married. An affair is not a solution," I said, trying not to sound too insensitive. "I mean, wouldn't your wife kill us both if she found out I stayed with you in a hotel room? Even if nothing happened, that just sounds... horrible!" I said, cringing at the thought. He seemed to cringe a little, too, and held his breath for a second.

"Yes, she would. But life is full of calculated risks. You win some, you lose some." He sipped his water. "Sometimes, it feels good to be bad." And with that statement, I knew he had definitely had an affair before.

I was silent. I honestly didn't know what to say, but I knew a "calculated risk" of this manner was something I wanted nothing to do with. A married man my Dad's age? No, thanks. House sitter was my title, not house wrecker! In that moment, I thought of sweet Pippa and I knew I would never see her again. And this conversation would be the last I would have with John. It was all too awkward to resolve. Ever.

I needed to get the heck out of there. I excused myself to go to the restroom just as the server brought our bill. I stayed in the restroom for about ten minutes longer than needed. I just wanted some time away from that table with John. It was stifling. One of my best clients propositioning me! Holy shit! I had to laugh so that I wouldn't lose it.

Underneath it all, I was mad at the whole situation. I felt bad for Pippa, for Glenda, and for their kids, whom I'd never met but had seen in photographs from birth to the present day framed all over their walls. I now knew a secret about someone's family that I didn't want to know. They seemed perfect, but now it was tainted by the realization that there were cracks in the foundation.

I arrived back at the table feeling drunker than when I left it, but I had to get out of there. I sat down, but before I could say anything John started.

"Is everything ok? You were gone a while, I was starting to wonder if you'd left me here." He laughed uncomfortably.

"It's…I'm fine," I said. "I'm ready to go. I think I'm OK to drive now," I lied.

"Are you sure? There's no rush." He seemed way too relaxed for the conversation I'd just endured.

"I'm sure." I got up from the table and grabbed my purse.

"Look, I know the last part of the night got a bit crazy, but can we please keep this between us? I think I am going to talk to Glenda and tell her how I have been feeling," he said. Something told me he had probably repeated those lines to others, and never said a peep to Glenda.

"Sure, OK," I said, feeling dizzy suddenly. I turned and headed toward the exit. He followed.

Once outside, he hugged me goodbye and I couldn't get to my car fast enough. I sat there in my car for almost an hour sobering up and replaying the dinner over and over in my head, still in shock.

In the months that followed, John and Glenda requested my services several times. I made up excuses each time so that I would never have to deal with the situation again. "I'm already booked," I'd say, or "I'm on vacation then," or, "I have friends in town," or, "I don't cover that area anymore"—all pretty solid excuses for a pet sitter, and sometimes they're even true. Eventually, they got the hint and stopped asking. They must have found some other pet sitter that suited their needs. Perhaps in more ways than one.

13
THE FIRST BITE IS THE DEEPEST

If there is one thing I guarantee every pet sitter has done besides clean up dog shit, pee and vomit, it is get bitten. Yes, a good ol' dog bite happens every now and then. I have been bitten three different times. It is not pleasant. It is not expected. I am lucky to still have all of my fingers and toes intact, and for that matter, my face.

As much as I love animals and prefer them to people, they can sometimes act a fool. Just like a crazy ex-boyfriend who, in an angry moment, flipped out and threw a glass at my wall, dogs too, can have their rare out-of-character moments. The good news is, 99% of the time they are non-aggressive toward humans they know and trust.

Most of the time trust is easy to establish between pet sitter and furry client. I typically have no issues. I know all the tricks: let them smell the back of your hand, get down to their level on the floor, and don't make eye contact at first. Also, let them smell, smell, smell to their heart's content. This soothes them (unless they smell a jerk). Treats can help too. Just meeting them where they are at on their terms is the best way to befriend a dog.

Notice I did not say cat. No. Cats will decide to claw your eyeball out on a dare from the voice in their head. Some cats are moody and fickle, which is a bad combination. I love cats, but they are liable to draw blood before you can even offer catnip. Never mistake a cat for a friendly-to-everyone dog; you will surely bleed to death, slowly, via deep claw marks. Cats demand space and respect like the Queen of England demands a good gin. Don't ask questions, just pour it. Don't get up in their business unless they invite you to, and even then, be wary.

Dogs demand respect too, but less of it. The one time you must not fuck with a dog is meal time. Have you ever heard the term "hangry"? It means hungry and angry, in other words, one gets angry when they are hungry. I do. I am pretty sure you do, too, and so do our furry friends. It is not a good idea to interfere with a dog's meal time. This means that sometimes you have to actually physically separate dogs from each other while they are eating. Yes, perfectly good doggie brothers and sisters turn into complete assholes when they are eating. Unfortunately, I learned this the hard way.

Sunny and Leah were the best dogs. They were well mannered and knew commands. Sunny was in his senior years, so he was a little crankier and at times noncompliant. Leah was several years younger and more playful. She didn't seem to care much about her food, and sometimes would get distracted and not finish her meal at breakfast time.

On this particular morning, Leah decided she wanted to dilly-dally with her food. Meanwhile, Sunny decided he was extra hungry, and instead of eating his food, he would abandon it halfway through and start on Leah's food, even though they ate the same kibble. I caught him heading her way and I walked over and put my foot down in is face to stop his head from going into her bowl.

Just like that, he growled and bit my foot, which was, unfortunately, in a flip-flop. Not the smartest shoe choice when interfering with animal meal time. My toe immediately started bleeding. He had drawn blood! I was stunned. I picked up Leah's food bowl since she wasn't eating it and I set it up on the counter so it wouldn't cause any more contention between them. I limped to the sink area and grabbed a paper towel to stop the gushing blood.

Luckily, upon further examination, there wasn't much trauma to my foot except for the broken skin between toes. I bandaged it up and never told the client. I decided it was my fault for being stupid and basically offering my foot during meal time.

Lesson learned.

———

The next time I got bit by a dog, I bawled like a toddler. It was pretty horrific. A great client of mine in Austin had decided to foster a little brindle-colored Dachshund mix. They were able to take their Poodle with them for the night but their foster dog was a bit skittish, and so they decided it best not to displace her. She was very well crate trained and they said I didn't need to go over more than a few times during the night and morning.

My clients left town in the early afternoon, so I arrived about 5:30 P.M. to give a potty break, treats, and dinner.   The rescue shelter had named her Rhonda. She looked like a real sweetie, but alas, looks can be deceiving. I let myself in and she was in a big wire crate in the corner, just as my client said she'd be. She was scrunched all the way in the back corner of the crate so I reached in and put some food in her bowl. She ate it timidly while I sat on the couch near her and checked my email on my phone.

After a few minutes, she was done. I clipped the leash to her collar and guided her out of her crate and outside. She sniffed around for a long time and finally did her business after about ten minutes. We slowly walked back inside, and I put her back into her crate and unhooked the leash. I left to meet a friend for dinner, planning to return around bedtime to give her another potty break.

The bedtime potty break was going well. I could tell Rhonda was terrified of me, other people outside, and pretty much everything in sight. She walked extremely slowly and cautiously. I did my best to be gentle and patient with her. After walking outside for what seemed like hours, she did her business on the lawn and we came back inside. I let her off the leash near the front door and figured she would dart into her crate. She ran and hid behind the dining table. I didn't know she could move so fast! I tried to coax her out from behind the table. I called her name and moved slowly. I even went down the hall to the bathroom for a minute to give her some time without me looming.

I came out of the bathroom expecting to find Rhonda in her crate, but she was still cowering behind the table. I decided I'd just need to pick her up and put her back into her crate at that point, or else we'd be playing this game for hours. I gently grabbed her around her chest and picked her up and out from behind the table. I was holding her close to me, her belly facing out. I took a few steps, and she jerked her head around to the side and bit me hard on the shoulder. I jerked her away from me as I shrieked in shock and pain, but retained my grip on her.

I set her down on the floor immediately to avoid getting another bite. She scurried off to her crate and I stood there and burst into tears, not out of pain but out of pity. What this poor dog must have gone through to become so terrified of even gentle strangers! I cried at the thought and rubbed my shoulder. It was red and starting to swell, but luckily no skin was broken. It hurt like hell! I quickly walked over to the crate and locked it for the night.

I returned for my last visit in the morning, and luckily that visit went more smoothly. I was extra careful with Rhonda and made sure to keep her leashed the entire time. My shoulder was black and blue. The strength in her little bite was fueled by her immense fear. My eyes got misty each time I thought about the abuse she might have endured prior to this foster care. She was deathly afraid of humans, even kind ones.

I never forgot about Rhonda and thought about her often. I asked my client about her a few months later. As it turns out, a couple of weeks after my visits with her she had darted out the front door and run away. They searched and called for her, but soon realized the efforts were futile. Rhonda was so petrified of everyone that she probably wouldn't answer to her name if called. So they stopped searching and hoped for the best.

"We're probably on the Austin Pets Alive foster care blacklist now," my client confessed.

It was then that I told them that Rhonda had bitten me out of pure fear. I could tell the client felt bad, but it was not their fault. Rhonda could have bitten anyone. Heck, she was so scared she could have bitten herself! Who knows whatever happened to her, poor little Rhonda.

———

Yet another time in I received a dog bite was while playing ball with a senior dog. Most dogs are happy to engage in a little "backyard ball," as I like to call it. It's a good way to give them some exercise without having to travel far like on a walk. It's great for older dogs who don't always have the stamina for a long walk, because in a backyard they can stop as soon as they get tired. I like to engage in backyard ball when rain or bad weather is threatening in Austin—it's an easy escape for cover into the house! I will usually wear latex gloves to throw the ball (I love dogs, but not their saliva!).

My client's dog, Peta, was crazy, and I mean *craaaazy*, about backyard ball. If I so much as picked up a tennis ball of hers lying somewhere in the house she would jump up with anticipation and fixate on me. She would play for hours if she could. Her eyes would glaze over and she'd get into the zone, seeing nothing but the tennis balls to be caught. I'd toss it over and over and over. She was relentless.

It had been raining for a few days, which was not conducive to a game of backyard ball. I didn't want to turn myself into a dog groomer and house cleaner simultaneously—cleaning mud off of her and everything in her path. So, we waited until it got drier out and the backyard was less muddy. She was so eager to get out and play after being pent up in the house. I grabbed some balls from her massive ball collection and we headed out back to play. She was squealing and wagging her tail frantically the whole way to the back door.

We played for about five minutes when I got a text message on my phone. I grabbed my phone off the patio table and looked at it as I picked up a ball she brought me to throw for the zillionth time. I picked up the ball which bounced at my feet from her mouth. I paused before throwing it so I could read the text I had just gotten, Peta was barking at me to get my attention. "Hold on Peta!" I said, not taking my eyes off of my phone screen. "Just a minute!" I said only half paying attention to her.

Then before I knew it I felt her teeth clenched on my hand. She had bitten my hand holding the ball! It throbbed in pain immediately. I was startled and looked at her with wide eyes. I threw the ball across the yard. I examined my hand, and luckily, she didn't draw blood, but it still hurt! We played a few more minutes of backyard ball and then went inside.

I needed to give Peta my full attention, and she had made sure I knew it. Dogs are serious about playtime! I never told the client because the bite could have been avoided if I was more engaged. Another black and blue mark, and another lesson learned.

14
WHERE'S THE FIRE?

One of the several questions I like to ask new clients is if there are any tricks to using their equipment. Any special instructions for your TV setup? Quirks with your sink or stove? Testy knobs or locks? Anything I should be aware of?

It's funny how every client thinks their TV setup is complicated. After dealing with all kinds over the years, I find very few TV setups too hard to manage. The TV system is the least of my problems. Usually, it is testy stoves or tricky knobs or locks I have the most trouble with.

One night I stood outside in the pouring rain, wrestling with a deadbolt lock for ten minutes because I knew that it was the only way in. The client's Great Dane would probably need to pee a river, and we both preferred that it occur outside. I couldn't reach the clients and I wouldn't give up on that deadbolt. It finally unlocked just when I was ready to give up and call a locksmith.

Another time and different clients, I was staying at Pat and Sue's house. After I'd cooked and eaten dinner, I retreated to the bedroom to take a shower. This was a drizzly day, and I was just going to shower, curl up on the couch, watch some TV, and call it a night.

About five minutes into my shower I heard a faint beeping, like an alarm of some sort. I listened intently and sure enough, there was an alarm going off. I rinsed the shampoo from my hair, wrapped it in a towel, and hurried out of the bedroom. The alarm got louder once I entered the living room. It was the security alarm panel. The fire alarm icon was flashing. I ran to the kitchen to grab the client's paperwork that had the security code. I punched it in and the alarm stopped.

My ears were ringing as I walked back to the bathroom in the master suite, feeling a bit on edge. I pulled the towel off of my head and got back in the shower to condition my hair. About five minutes had passed when I heard the dogs barking crazily. *What now?* I wondered. I hurried and finished my shower so I could get out and see what all the fuss was about. I wrapped my hair in the towel and wrapped another towel around my chest so it hung just far enough to cover the important parts.

I could hear men's voices as I rounded the corner to the living room, and before I could turn around there were three firemen standing in front of me. I wanted to scream, but no sound would come out. The dogs had begun sniffing them all over while I stood there frozen, clutching the skimpy towel around me.

A clean-cut fireman in his thirties was calmly petting one of the dogs on the head "Sorry to startle you ma'am, but there was a fire alarm alert indicated at this address. Is everything OK?" The other two firefighters looked away politely. The red emergency lights from the fire truck out front reflected through the living room windows and swirled on the walls and the sides of their faces.

An actual fire truck was out there in the street idling loudly. This was just great. *God knows what the neighbors are thinking*, I thought to myself.

"Um, well, the fire alarm on the security panel was going off, but I don't know why. There wasn't any fire. I just finished cooking dinner a while ago, and I ate and then jumped in the shower. That is when it went off," I said, feeling silly. "How did you get in?" I asked, hoping there wasn't damage somewhere that I'd have to repair or explain to my client.

"We have a specially designed magnet tool we use to unlock deadbolts. That way we don't have to destroy doors if a place isn't visibly on fire," he explained. "We were mainly worried about these guys." He looked down at the dogs, who were completely oblivious to how awkward the situation was. I wished I were.

"Since there is not a fire, this will be considered a false alarm and will be filed with your alarm company. The City may charge you for it if it happens more than once," he said.

"Well, I'm house sitting—this is not my house," I blurted out. "I don't know if it has happened before, but I will make sure to leave the homeowner a note," I said.

"Great. Sorry to startle you. We just wanted to be sure everyone was OK, and we could hear the dogs barking," he said as they turned to exit.

"Thank you for that, and I'm sorry about the false alarm!" I said, relieved that they were heading out.

I shut the door behind them and I wanted until I heard the loud truck roar down the street. I headed back to the bedroom to change and get ready for bed.

Four hours later, in the wee hours of the morning, it happened again. The fire alert on the security panel sounded. It woke me out of a deep sleep and I flew out of bed and ran into the living room to the security panel. I remembered the code from earlier and was able to get it to shut off quickly. I hoped the fire truck wouldn't make another appearance. This had to stop! Risking electrocution, I dismantled the alarm panel down to the wires for any visible signs causing it to malfunction. It seemed perfectly fine. I reassembled it and returned to bed.

Two nights later it happened again. Unfortunately, my clients were in the Bali jungle and I was unable to reach them. This was before cell phones were easy to use on an international vacation.

I had emailed them, and they simply said they would have it checked out as soon as they arrived back in the States.

I was beyond frustrated, and I decided that this would be the last time I'd pet sit for them. The fact that they likely knew it was malfunctioning prior to my stay, and neglected to inform me, really rubbed me the wrong way. How could they give me the alarm code and forget to mention that it was temperamental?

This is something one occasionally runs into when pet sitting. As you read in chapter four, a client's heater completely stopped working in the dead of winter mere days after he departed for his trip. This spurred a string of events that would almost prove fatal for my pet sitting career. Sometimes things go wrong. Sometimes *everything* goes wrong. Sometimes clients want so badly to get away on vacation, they forget to ensure that all the house functions are operating correctly. Or sometimes they don't forget, but they just don't care. In their minds, they're already on a beach in Bora Bora.

How do you know when you badly need a vacation? It is when you think, "She'll figure it out." No, I probably won't figure it out. I'm a pet sitter. I'm not an electrician, or a locksmith, or a plumber, last I checked. I'm also not deaf to the piercing sound of fire alarms going off.

EPILOGUE

You might find it amusing that this book was almost named, "The Good News Is, I didn't Burn Your House Down," but when the silver-lining of a pet sitting job is that someone's home is still upright, that is a dismal situation. I thought better of such a catastrophic title, although funny (and true).

"I Had Sex in Your Bed and Other Things Only Your Dog Knows," was another title contender, but I soon realized that the first question people will ask me for the rest of my life is: Did you really have sex in your client's bed? My answer would be, "Buy the book." However, I really didn't want to have to come up with an obligatory chapter about my sex life. So that was out.

If pet sitting has taught me anything, it is that life is unpredictable. Pet sitting isn't rocket science, but it is very easy to screw-up! I believe my growing passion for animals helped me build up resilience for these screw-ups along the way. I've learned that generosity, conscientiousness, a positive attitude and a loving nature sets the tone for success with clients, their animals, or anyone I interact with in daily life.

If I was hanging out with animals simply for a paycheck, the events in the chapters you've just read would have undoubtedly steered me quickly away from pet care. These experiences have tested me in ways I never expected, but for every less-than-stellar pet sitting situation I've had, I've probably had forty fantastic ones. I've found this business personally fulfilling in a way that sitting behind a desk in a corporate office never was.

The past fifteen years have made me a more capable pet sitter, and a stronger person. I have honed my focus and have become more dependable, respectful, aware, unassuming, conscientious, responsible and confident. I believe those traits are what separate the professionals from the amateurs!

Believe it or not, I've pet sat for free and I've also spent the night teetering on one butt cheek on the edge of a client's bed so I wouldn't disturb their pets who were deep asleep sprawled out on the bed next to me. That is to say, I truly do care about animals. When I say, "Thank you for choosing me," in my welcome-home letter to clients returning from vacation, I mean it.

Will I pet sit as a profession forever? Probably not. My beloved Miniature Pinscher, Jiminey Cricket, passed away not long ago and I want to be a pet owner again someday and get some dogs or cats of my own.

I only hope that when I go on vacation and hire a pet sitter that I won't end up in a chapter of a book like this one day.

ACKNOWLEDGMENTS

I would like to thank my twin sister, Kellie Tomlin, for giving me my first opportunity to pet sit (for her coworker) many years ago. If someone would have told me I'd still be doing it all these years later, I wouldn't have believed them.

This is for all of the pets and pet owners I have served, thank you. This book would not have been possible without you.

I would like to thank my family and friends for your love, support and encouragement. You empowered me to go all the way with this book. Thank you for believing in me.

This book would have taken a lot longer to publish if it wasn't for the love, support, and encouragement of Aaron Husak. Thanks for listening to me drone on about it for the past few years.

I learned that it takes a village to publish a book! A special thanks goes out to those individuals (even those not listed here) who helped me with editing, cover design and other writing related processes: My editor, Adam O'Brien, Joanna Penn, Mark Dawson, Carol Rushing, Danita Mayer, Swati Hegde, John Gorman, Jennifer Leach, Christina Alexandra, Donna Rivera and designer Iva23.

ABOUT THE AUTHOR

Yvonne M. Feltman aspires to be a New York Times bestselling author.

A former executive assistant, Yvonne relocated to Austin, Texas in 2013 from Albuquerque, New Mexico. After working in the corporate world for nearly fifteen years, she decided to change direction in 2015 when she quit her job to pursue writing and other interests.

Yvonne is an independent copywriter and ghostwriter writing for various websites and publications. She also owns a successful pet sitting company in Austin, Texas called Custom Critter Sitters, LLC.

Yvonne has been writing since she was in middle school. She enjoys creating stories and connecting with others through words. When she is not writing or frolicking with other's pets, Yvonne enjoys cooking and trying new restaurants, running and outdoor activities, listening to music and dancing, listening to podcasts, reading, and learning.

To contact Yvonne, or to find out more information, visit her online at **www.yvonnefeltman.com**

Author's Note: If you enjoyed this book, please take a moment to write a simple one-sentence review. Thank you for reading!

27579370R00089

Made in the USA
San Bernardino, CA
01 March 2019